CF-GBY

CF-GBY

WARDAIR

D0336397

£3.95

Below: Seen at altitude just inland from the Dutch coast, the first F-16B Fighting Falcon for the Royal Netherlands Air Force, J-259. *RNethAF*

aircraft
ILLUSTRATED
Annual 1982

Edited by
Martin Horseman

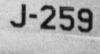

LONDON

IAN ALLAN LTD

First published 1981

ISBN 0 7110 1134 6

Published by Ian Allan Ltd, Shepperton, Surrey;
and printed by Ian Allan Printing Ltd at their works
at Coombelands in Runnymede, England

Below: **Three RAF Avro 679 Rota I autogyros seen during a flight from Old Sarum, Wilts in 1935.** *RAF Museum, Charles E. Brown collection*

Contents

SMILE PLEASE!

MICHAEL TURNER

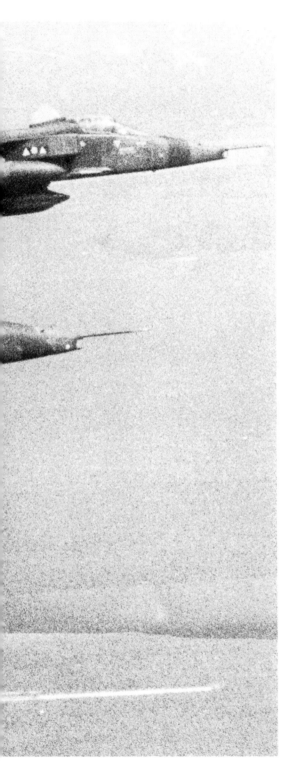

IN APRIL 1976, No 2 Squadron RAF started operating the Sepecat Jaguar in the tactical reconnaissance role; the squadron is a component of the RAF Germany forces assigned to NATO's Supreme Allied Commander Europe (SACEUR) and under the direct control of the Commander, 2 ATAF (Second Allied Tactical Air Force). The nature of the job is one of hide-and-seek; and it demands the ability to intrude over 'enemy' territory in time of conflict without being detected, to observe and photograph troop movements, deployment, concentration and strength — and to get the information and film back to base. Of necessity the task involves flying constantly fast and very low, making maximum use of cover afforded by valleys, wooded hillsides, and any other natural feature available. It is therefore unusual to find the squadron's Jaguars flying at altitudes above 500ft, and a good deal of their time airborne is spent considerably lower than this.

The Jaguar GR1 in its photo-reconnaissance guise carries a recce-pod on the centre-line stores point, with additional fuel tanks on the inner wing pylons and cluster bombs on the outer ones. The recce-pod houses a 'fan' camera, which scans a 180° arc from horizon to horizon, and a fixed camera in the nose; as the use of the latter involves the alignment of the aircraft with the photo target, the pilots have to develop the considerable ability to point their aircraft accurately at the area they wish to record, and to do so in the split second available between sighting the target and passing it by at 500 knots or so. He is unlikely to get a second opportunity. The pod also has an Infra Red Line Scan (IRLS) facility housed at the rear, and this is used for photographing tactical units under camouflage or in wooded areas, as well as being excellent at night.

Under operational conditions, the Squadron can be tasked by 2 ATAF for Air Force intelligence requirements, or by the Commander NORTHAG (Northern Army Group) for Army Intelligence. Both of these Commands assess the priorities of their various unit's requests, and pass these through Wings to the Squadron, which then tasks its individual aircraft for specific missions.

On receipt of a task, the selected pilot is given a provisional briefing on the target and information required, the positions of known concentrations of

Left: **Seen against the hazy conditions encountered during the first sector of the author's sortie, the two accompanying Jaguar GR1s track past an autobahn over-bridge.**
All photos in this article by the author

5

Above: **Groundcrew removing a reconnaissance pod from its centreline station beneath a No 2 Squadron Jaguar GR1, XZ107/R, at RAF Laarbruch.**

Right: **Film from a Jaguar reconnaissance sortie laid out on a light table in the RIC, where a photo interpreter is seen completing a post-flight report.**

hostile forces en route, etc, and he then works out his own flight plan, fuel load, and the other parameters of the sortie. Immediately before setting out, he receives an update on the target situation, and with the aircraft readied for the task, the mission is dispatched. Having reached the target, photographed it and assessed the situation, the pilot radios a visual report to Wing or Army Corps as soon as he leaves the target area, and this is considered while the aircraft is returning to base with pictures, which are expected to confirm the pilot's report to within very close limits. If possible, the pilot will also pass a radio report to the Division or Battle Group directly concerned during his return flight. On arrival at its base airfield, the aircraft taxys directly to its HAS (Hardened Aircraft Shelter), the armament is made safe, and it is pushed into the shelter, after which the engines are shut down, and the film containers extracted from the pod. These are passed to a waiting motor cyclist, who rushes the exposed

Above: **Night time view of a HAS with two Jaguars securely housed inside.**

film to the RIC (Reconnaissance Intelligence Centre), where it is processed at the rate of 100ft/min, dried, and laid out on a light table to be assessed with the aid of a stereoscope by a photo-interpreter — this evaluation of the film is normally possible within 5 minutes of its receipt at the RIC. The information gleaned is then passed to Command to supplement and confirm the pilot's earlier visual report, and the necessary follow-up action is initiated.

No 2 Squadron has been a specialist photo-reconnaissance unit since its formation on 12 May 1912. Among the Squadron's notable early achievements, it provided the first British pilot to land on French soil in WW1, and carried out the first wartime reconnaissance sortie on 20 August 1914. The role has been developed over the years, and between the wars No 2's theatre of operations spread from Southern Ireland to Shanghai. In WW2, the Squadron's expertise was directed mainly in the European theatre, and, ever since its basing near Antwerp following the Allied landings in 1944, it has been stationed on the Continent. Deservedly proud of their enviable reputation, the Squadron, at present commanded by Wg Cdr Tim Thorn, consistently comes out top among its NATO partners in air exercises and in SACEUR's annual Tactical Evaluations.

The principal purpose of my recent visit to No 2 Squadron's base at RAF Laarbruch was to fly a photo-sortie and secure pictures and first-hand impressions of the aircraft in its operational environment; and to this end I was to be slotted into the rear seat of one of the 2-seat Jaguar T2s. The T2 would fly 'chase' with two GR1 single-seaters, the

sortie being scheduled for a 12.30 hrs take-off, and recovery at 14.00 hrs. My pilot was to be Sqn Ldr Ron Elder, the Squadron second-in-command, and our fellow travellers, to be photographed on this trip instead of doing the picture-taking themselves, were Flt Lts Dick Shuster and Chris Daymon in the pair of GR1s.

The weather for the trip was sunny and hot, though very hazy, as is normal for the area I was advised. I spent the morning being kitted-out and fitted to a parachute harness, a fairly punishing physical experience in itself, as the body (mine) had to be tightly trussed-up to cope with the stresses of a possible ejection. Any slack in the 'system' could otherwise cause the harness to slip out of place and probably do more harm than good to the unfortunate wearer (me again). The fitting involved much fierce and violent tugging and pulling on the various straps and laces, until one's torso is so compressed as to render normal breathing something of an effort. The whole process was performed with apparent relish by one Cpl Farman in the flying clothing stores, who probably considered me fair game — on a par with his normal clientele! Packaged-up to his evident satisfaction, I made a strangely distorted attempt at walking to the Mini-van for transportation to the harness rig, from which I was to be 'hung' to test the fit and ensure, firstly, that my body would not slip from the iron grip of the harness under the shock of a parachute opening, and, secondly, probably an incidental consideration, that the chances of damage to the more important parts of the anatomy were reduced to a minimum.

Having successfully completed 'the drop', and been fitted with a bone-dome, I was all set. But with an hour still to go before take-off, I decided to keep the harness on lest I should be unable to compress my frame into it again at the given time. Consequently, as the kit is presumably intended to be acceptably uncomfortable in a sitting posture but not in a vertical one, I continued to hobble around like Quasimodo looking for a lost coin on the ground.

A little after Noon, following an half-hearted attempt at a couple of sandwiches, we walked to the aircraft and went through the usual strapping-in procedures, and I stowed my various additional pieces of photographic equipment. The rear seat of the Jaguar T2 really does afford an excellent field of view compared to that from some other two-seaters, and there was enough elbow room for the handling of the two 35mm cameras I slung round my neck. I would have preferred to have had only one camera to grapple with, but as we were destined to remain airborne for 1½ hr, I did not want to risk a camera malfunction with no back-up as this would have been acutely embarrassing, to say the least.

Lined-up on Laarbruch's runway, we let the pair of single-seaters go first before starting our roll, climbing out at only a shallow angle after take-off to some 500ft. Flt Lt Shuster had been left to plan our route, incorporating as many and varied backdrops as possible during our allotted time, and this very experienced pilot was to ensure that I would not be short of workload. As predicted, the atmosphere was very hazy, but we expected it to clear as we headed towards our first objective, the famous Mohne Dam. I had switched on the head-up display and terrain-following map/radar but as soon as the haze cleared I concentrated on some air-to-airs, against a rich backdrop of dark wooded hills. We popped up to 3,000ft briefly to see how effectively the other aircraft merged into the landscape when viewed from above as they darted between the contours of the ground, then down again to tuck in alongside. In no time it seemed we were running in low to the Dam, rocketing between the twin towers made famous by the Dambusters 36 years ago. I fired off a quick burst from my camera with the help of a power-winder, and we were away and heading for our next target, an

Below: **Lined-up on the Laarbruch runway, the pair of single-seaters with Flt Lts Dick Shuster and Chris Daymon about to roll for a formation take-off.**

Above left: **The T2, flown by Sqn Ldr Ron Elder, No. 2 Squadron's 2i/c, tucks in astern of the two GR1s outbound from RAF Laarbruch.**

Left: **A port-side view of the two GR1s in close company against a backdrop of pastures and arable land.**

Below: **The panorama switches to wooded country intersected by another autobahn.**

inevitable but nonetheless impressive shot of the pair passing below the walls of a typically romantic *Schloss*. We hunted out some 'Brown Jobs' on manoeuvres, complete with what are apparently known as 'Grunt Vehicles', and an Army camp or two, before tracking zig-zag between the wooded slopes of a river valley to emerge, my senses reeling, over more open country again, heading North now towards Cologne. In spite of the air-conditioning, which was turned up full at my request, I was working up a considerable body temperature from the effort of juggling with my cameras and resisting the incipient 'g' forces, and from past experience I knew that, 45 minutes into the flight, I would probably soon be grappling for one of the plastic bags placed within easy 'reach' (sorry — grasp) in my flying suit.

We got in some more shots as we sped past a large monument in some hills, before I succumbed to the rigours of flying in a military jet and examined the

inside of bag No 1 which had temporarily assumed a greater importance than all the other fascinating things going on around me. There was time to change a couple of films, which gave me a breathing space while straight and level, before a call to air traffic gave us the opportunity to rocket past the control tower of Cologne's city airport — at an impressive height straight down the main runway. On our return leg to base, we got in some more air-to-airs as we shot past railway bridges, Rhine barges, Army camps and missile sites, and had our picture taken by Dick Shuster's pod mounted camera. We turned in over the threshold alongside Chris Daymon, and kept alongside as he did a touch-and-go on the runway for some more pictures, then around the circuit to line up again on the runway, turning tightly in view of the proximity of the Dutch border and local noise-abatement requirements; and then we were down.

Back at the HAS, the delight of releasing the canopy to the always welcome wave of fresh, cool air, the unbuckling of the multitude of straps, pipes and connectors to release me from the grip of 23,000lb of metal and brute force, down the steps from my lofty perch and the reassuring comfort of terra-firma. Looking back now at the photo taken as we stood casually at the foot of the steps, I can't help noticing that I look a shade greener than my steely-eyed and grinning companions, and I can tell you that the hue was not due to envy on my part!

Below: **A No 2 Squadron pilot fills in some post-flight paperwork before leaving his aircraft parked outside its HAS.**

Above: **Derby Airways was the passenger and freight carrying division of Derby Aviation Ltd, a company with its roots buried deep in the wartime rush to provide training schools for RAF navigators and pilots. The airline operation emerged in 1948 and adopted ex-service Dakotas as the mainstay of its fleet, quickly building a flourishing business on the popular routes from regional airports in the Midlands to the Channel Islands. By 1961, up to eight Dakotas were carrying the Derby colours across Europe and down into the holiday areas of the Mediterranean. Three years later the company had outgrown its early localised image, and its expanding field of operations led to the acquisition of its first turbine equipment and a change of name to the more representative British Midland Airways.**

All photos by the author unless otherwise credited

INDEPENDENT
Dakotas

PETER GILCHRIST

Above: Formed as it was in 1948, Starways was one of the earliest post-war independent airlines. It was originally a charter specialist but began to fly scheduled services from its Liverpool base in 1955. Routes were opened to London, Glasgow and Manchester, a number of regional centres, and various continental airports. The company used several Dakotas during its formative years and these aircraft were the nucleus of its fleet until the early-1960s. During 1963 Starways was taken over by British Eagle International and a new company — British Eagle (Liverpool) Ltd — was formed to accommodate the route licences previously held by Starways. Although a separate company, it was always very much a Northern Division of the Heathrow-based parent, and when money ran out for British Eagle International in November 1968, the 'kids from Liverpool' were killed off in the stampede.

Below: With its operational base at the centre of a popular holiday area, tedious sea crossings as its main competition during the lean winter months, and positive taxation advantages over mainland-based carriers, Jersey Airlines was all set for a bright future when it began operations way back in 1948. Routes were quickly opened to London and Paris, as well as to regional centres on both sides of the Channel. Originally equipped with Rapides and Herons, the airline grew rapidly during the 1950s and added a substantial number of Dakotas to its fleet at the end of the decade. November 1962 saw a second major re-grouping of British independent operators, and Jersey Airlines combined with Manx Airlines Ltd and the northern interests of Silver City Airways, to become part of the British United Airways group. After amalgamation, the new airline became BUA(CI) Ltd, and remained so until its name was changed to British United Island Airways (BUIA) in October 1968. When the parent British United Airways joined forces with Caledonian to form British Caledonian Airways in 1970, BUIA remained outside the main consortium and changed its name once more to become British Island Airways (BIA).

Top: **Channel Airways began operations shortly after the war as East Anglian Flying Services. Based at Southend, the company quickly realised that its future lay in international services and increasingly linked Britain's coastal towns with Europe and the Channel Islands. Imaginative use of express coaches through major population centres gave passengers an easy access to regional airports such as Ipswich, Rochester and Portsmouth. Air services were operated to Holland, Belgium, France and Spain with a fleet of twenty or so aircraft, including seven Dakotas. After the early years of vigorous growth, Channel began to convert to turbine equipment with the acquisition of seven ex-BEA Viscount 701s in 1964. These were quickly followed by second-hand Comets, and a fleet of new HS748s, Tridents and BAC One-Elevens. This outward show of affluence and success concealed an enormous problem of increasing unit-costs and declining utilisation. The Tridents were disposed of during 1971 in an attempt to reduce fleet diversity, and some services were cancelled to cut costs. The 'rescue' operation came too late: Channel fell into deep financial trouble during the winter of 1971-72, finally calling in a receiver and going into liquidation — a victim of increasing competition.**

Above: **BKS Air Transport was formed in February 1952 by Messrs Barnby, Keegan and Stevens. Operating from Southend, with secondary bases at Leeds and Newcastle, the company quickly developed into one of the most efficient independent airlines in the UK. Within three years it had secured a small system of scheduled routes, entered the fields of trooping and inclusive-tour charters, and developed a successful freight business with a fleet of five Dakotas and three Vikings. The company was one of a carefully selected group of independent airlines 'mothered' by British European Airways, and had attracted a 30% shareholding from the Corporation by the early-1960s. During the mid-1960s a number of these 'associate' arrangements were shed by the Corporation but BKS was chosen for further development, along with Cambrian Airways. A new company called British Air Services (70% owned by BEA) was set up in 1967 to ensure the financial integrity of the two independents, both of which continued to operate under their original names. BKS became Northeast Airlines — still under the BAS banner — during 1970, and continued to use that name until British Airways was formed in 1972. At that time both independent identities were lost as the two BAS airlines were fully absorbed into the parent company.**

Below: In common with BKS Air Transport, Cambrian Airways was under the management guidance of British European Airways for some years before being fully absorbed into British Airways during 1972. Although Cambrian was formed way back in 1935, it did not initiate scheduled services until 1948. Based in Cardiff, it concentrated most ot its early flying on Wales and the West of England, linking these areas with the Channel Islands and the major industrial regions of the UK; international services were available to Paris, Dinard, Dublin and Cork. In 1956 the airline signed a ten-year operating agreement with BEA and took over all of the Corporation's Irish Sea services. Two years later BEA acquired a 30% shareholding in the airline, and began a process that would eventually lead to Cambrian becoming a wholly owned subsidiary of British Air Services before losing its individual identity altogether in 1972.

Right: Dan-Air was formed in the spring of 1953 and its name reflected its position as a wholly owned subsidiary of Davies & Newman Ltd, a well established firm of shipping brokers. Operations began with a single Dakota (G-AMSU) bought from Meredith Air Transport in June 1953, and a second was added to the inventory during the following February. After some years of charter work with the two Dakotas and a number of ex-RAF Yorks, the company initiated scheduled services during the summer of 1956 and steadily consolidated its position as one of the major independent airlines in the UK. This aircraft, G-AMPP, was the third Dakota acquired by Dan-Air, having come from Scottish Airlines in 1961 after seeing service with the RAF as KK135. The aircraft is now preserved at Lasham – the airline's maintenance headquarters in Hampshire – painted to represent the original Dan-Air Dakota, G-AMSU.

Above: **Silver City Airways is best remembered for its pioneering work on vehicle/passenger air ferry services using the Bristol 170-series Freighters but it was also very much involved with scheduled passenger services, particularly those linking Blackpool with other regional airports and the Continent. G-AMWV,** *City of Lancaster,* **was one of a number of Dakotas owned by the airline at the time of its incorporation into British United Airways during November 1962. The complete air ferry operation was combined with Channel Air Bridge — already a British United company — to form British United Air Ferries, while the northern regional passenger services were teamed-up with those of Jersey Airlines to form BUA (CI) Ltd.** *Hugh Newell*

Below: **Air Links started operations in 1959 with a single Dakota and eventually progressed to an all 4-engined fleet of ex-BOAC Hermes and Argonaut aircraft. After a fresh injection of capital during 1966, the airline's name was changed to Transglobe Airways Ltd and two Britannias were bought for long-range charter operations. Dakota G-APUC (c/n 12893, ex-EI-ACH) was acquired from Aer Lingus during May 1959 and spent the major part of its life on long-term charter work in Africa. It was finally sold to Royal Nepal Airlines as 9N-AAM, leaving Gatwick for the last time on 5 April 1964. Transglobe Airways ran into financial trouble during 1968; it ceased operations in November of that year and went into liquidation shortly afterwards.**

Top: Encouraged by a little ministerial pressure during the late-1950s, Britain's two major long-range independent airlines — the Airwork Group and Hunting Clan — joined forces during July 1960 to become British United Airways. The government-inspired 'big is beautiful' campaign was a political manoeuvre to ease the task of apportioning new, low-fare licences to Africa between BOAC and the independent airlines. The early partners in this new venture were subsequently joined by a number of smaller airlines, including the northern interests of Silver City Airways, and Jersey Airlines. Between them, these new partners brought nine additional Dakotas into the group, increasing the overall fleet commitment to a maximum of 16 during 1961-62. Further changes within the group resulted in the two new members being merged into a separate operating division, to be known as British United (Channel Islands) Ltd. The majority of BUA Dakotas were used by this new division, but for a short period only: 1961 saw the arrival in Jersey of the first of a fleet of new Handley Page Heralds. British United Airways finally merged

with Caledonian Airways during November 1970, to begin the process that would lead to the formation of the present-day British Caledonian Group. The Jersey based subsidiary remained outside this new grouping, to become British Island Airways during 1970.

Above: British Westpoint Airlines was an Exeter-based subsidiary of Metropolitan Air Movements. Formed as a charter operator in 1961, the airline went into scheduled flying on 7 May 1962 when it opened a daily service between London (Heathrow) and Exeter, using two ex-BEA Dakotas. This route was initially extended to Newquay, and then other services began to link Heathrow and Gatwick with Plymouth, Bristol, Cardiff and Ostend. With the existing fleet fully extended, a third Dakota — also from BEA — was acquired during late-February 1963. After taking over Mayflower Air Services in 1964 and absorbing their fleet of DH Rapides, Westpoint seemed to lose direction and finally ceased operations in May 1966.

17

ANNALS of the AUTOGYRO

R.A. NICHOLLS

AT A time when the RAF has been taking delivery of the Boeing-Vertol Chinook HC1 for service in the medium-lift helicopter role, the RAF Museum has revived memories of the mid-1930s by selecting as the latest aircraft exhibit to go on display at Hendon a machine which recalls the RAF's first faltering steps along the path of rotary-winged aviation. The aircraft in question is not a helicopter, but an Avro 671 Rota I autogyro, serial number K4232, dating from 1934; the Rota I was an Avro-built example of the civil Cierva C30A, and at the time of its entry into service it represented the last word in autogyro technology.

Below: **Cierva C19 MkIV, G-ABUF, photographed on take-off; note the stub wings for mounting the ailerons.** Flight, *via the author*

In the early-1920s several designers were actively investigating the potential of rotary-winged flight as a means of overcoming the problems of stalling associated with fixed-wing aircraft. In the autogyro the rotor blades, which are of aerofoil section and set at a shallow positive pitch angle, typically some 3° to the plane of rotation, are not engine-driven but are free to 'autorotate'; as the aircraft moves forward on the ground under the influence of the propeller the rotor assembly starts to rotate due to the slipstream, thus generating lift and causing the machine to rise into the air. As long as forward speed is maintained the rotor will continue to autorotate and produce lift; should forward speed start to decrease, either by design or otherwise, the machine will commence a steady descent. The resultant upward airflow, however, will cause autorotation to be maintained and lift to be generated; this lift, while not sufficient to prevent further loss of altitude, will allow the machine to make a safe descent to earth, even with a dead engine.

Pre-eminent in the field of autogyro design was the Spanish engineer Juan de la Cierva. Cierva's first three machines, built during the years 1920-22, were all unsuccessful owing to the use of rigid rotors; as the rotor turns through the air the blades generate more lift during the forward half of the revolution, when the aerofoil section is moving into the airstream, than on the reverse part of the cycle, when it is moving downstream. The practical effect of this lift differential is to cause the blades to rise and fall alternately as they go through the forward and reverse parts of each revolution, and the use of rigid rotors permitted this imbalance to be transmitted to the whole aircraft in the form of a turning moment, imparting a rolling motion and making the machine dangerously unstable. To overcome this problem Cierva introduced flap hinges at the blade attachment points on the rotor head, thus allowing each blade to move vertically, within limits, independently of the others, and so preventing the unequal lift forces from affecting the stability of the machine as a whole. This principle was employed by Cierva on his first successful design, the C4, which made its maiden flight at Getafe, near Madrid on 9 January 1923, the design being based on an Hanriot aircraft and Le Rhone 9Ja rotary engine.

It should be mentioned that for the sake of simplicity the term 'autogyro' is used here to describe any aircraft which derives its lift from an autorotating rotor system, the rotor not being engine-driven in flight. In fact, when Cierva achieved success with the C4 he had the name 'Autogiro' registered as a trade name for machines using rotor systems of his design, and in order to be strictly correct one should use the word autogyro as a generic term for this type of aircraft, while Cierva types should be referred to as Autogiros. Having established the clear distinction between these two terms, so often a cause of confusion, the former will continue in this instance to include all types.

That Cierva's first successful design was based on an Hanriot aircraft illustrates the most common method of autogyro construction at that time, namely the application of a Cierva rotor system to an established and proven fixed-wing aircraft, suitably modified. Among the types most commonly used were the Avro 504 and Avian, the 504 being particularly popular and forming the basis of Cierva's C6 and C8 series of machines. The C6, the first two seat autogyro, was widely demonstrated in 1926-27, frequently by Cierva himself, and proved to be an initial success by the standards of the time. Accidents were, however, commonplace at that early stage and each was thoroughly investigated in order to isolate the cause, the knowledge thus gained being applied in the next stage of development — autogyro research was very much a process of trial and error, and progress was slow but sure. Two recurring sources of trouble were fatigue failure of the blades at the attachment points and the troublesome phenomenon known as 'ground resonance'. It was to overcome fatigue failure that drag hinges, also known as lag hinges, were introduced in 1926, permitting a degree of independent fore and aft movement in each blade in addition to the vertical freedom afforded by the flap hinges already described. The first design to incorporate both types of hinge was Cierva's C8, another two seater, the Lynx-engined C8L version of which became the first rotary-winged aircraft to fly across the English Channel when, on 18 September 1928, Cierva himself flew G-EBYY from London (Croydon) to Paris (Le Bourget), carrying as passenger the editor of a leading French aeronautical journal. After arrival at Paris the machine was taken by Cierva and his recently-recruited test pilot, A. H. Rawson, on a European demonstration tour, visiting Brussels, Berlin, and Amsterdam before returning to Paris where G-EBYY was handed over to Cierva's French licensees, Weymann-Lepere, for experimental use before being donated to the *Musee de l'Air*, where she remains to this day. Ground resonance, for many years the bane of autogyro designers everywhere, was the result of the rotor assembly's centre of gravity not coinciding with the geometric centre, resulting in an out-of-balance condition and consequent vibration. This condition might result from a static imbalance between the individual blades, but was more commonly due to the centre of gravity moving away from the geometric centre as blades flexed during rotation; operation of the rotor system in an unbalanced condition would

Above: **The Cierva C6C, J8068, being demonstrated during the Hendon Air Display in 1926.** *Imperial War Museum, via the author*

result in severe oscillation of the fuselage and, if the machine was on the ground, would tend to increase in severity until the machine finally broke up or rolled over onto its side. The fitment of 'drag dampers' to damp out unstable movements of the drag hinges and keep the blades in the right positions relative to one another went a long way towards maintaining the centre of gravity and preventing ground resonance, but it continued to rear its head from time to time and was the downfall of many autogyro designs throughout the 1920s and 1930s.

Since the autogyro's rotor system was at this time solely to provide lift, moveable control surfaces had to be retained. The ailerons were generally mounted on a pair of outriggers, the original mainplanes no longer being required, although some early designs did make use of stub wings to mount the ailerons and also to provide a small amount of lift, thus relieving the rotor of some of the loading whilst the machine was moving at speed. In most cases the tail unit was orthodox and remained fundamentally the same as on the original fixed-wing aircraft.

Cierva, who had formed a British company, the Cierva Autogiro Co Ltd, at Hamble in 1926, involved himself chiefly in design and development matters, tending to leave the actual construction in the hands of other companies who built under licence, using Cierva rotor systems on machines of their own or Cierva's design. Among the companies so engaged were Avro, Parnall, De Havilland, and Westland in the UK; Kellett and Pitcairn in the US; Weymann-Lepere and Liore et Olivier in France; Focke-Wulf in Germany; and the Kayaba Industrial Company in Japan. By far the closest and strongest association was with the Avro Company, which had a drawing office and manufacturing facility at Hamble where they built many of the Cierva designs.

Prior to 1929 all autogyros employed manual turning of the rotor assembly, by means of a rope wound around the rotor head, at the start of the take-off run in order to assist in the attainment of autorotation and reduce the length of run needed to get airborne but the C19 Mk 1, exhibited at the 1929 Olympia Aero Show, incorporated a novel feature aimed at doing away with this cumbersome procedure. The C19 Mk 1's tail unit consisted of a box-like structure of twin tailplanes mounted in biplane style with a fin and rudder at each end; with the machine stationary on the ground the tail unit could be tilted forward through nearly 90° and the engine run up, the propeller slipstream being deflected upwards by the tail unit and causing the rotor to turn and gather speed whereupon, sufficient rotor speed having been built up, the tail unit was restored to its normal position and take-off effected, the rotor continuing in autorotation. Crude that this method may have been, it was nonetheless a significant step forward since it freed the autogyro from the need for a ground party to carry out the laborious ritual of rotor turning, and this relative ease of operation added considerably to the machine's appeal and increased its sales potential, particularly in the field of club and private operators.

Three years later the slipstream deflection method of rotor starting was itself overtaken by the introduction of a mechanism, designed by the Armstrong Siddeley Co, whereby an auxiliary drive was taken from the rear of the engine crankshaft, via a clutch, and made to turn the rotor by means of a vertical drive shaft carrying a bevel pinion; this pinion meshed with a crown-wheel at the rotor head in order to run the rotor up to speed before take-off. With the wheel brakes applied and the aircraft facing into wind the drive clutch to the mechanism was engaged and the throttle opened, the resultant rotor speed being one-eighth that of the crankshaft due to the use of a reduction gear; the rotor was run up to between 180 and 210rpm depending on wind strength, whereupon the drive clutch was disengaged, the wheel brakes released, and the throttle opened fully. With the control column eased back the machine would lift off in about 30yd, at an airspeed of some 25mph, and the rotor would continue in autorotation. This system was tested and proved on the C19 Mk IV, which reverted to a more orthodox tail unit, the slipstream deflection feature being no longer required. A total of 29 machines of the C19 series were produced and, apart from the UK, saw service in Spain, Germany, Sweden and the Far East; in the UK two examples were purchased by the Air Ministry while several others went to private operators, including Alan (later Sir Alan) Cobham's Flying Circus.

The bulk of the Avro facility was transfered to Manchester in 1928-29, leaving only a nucleus of draughtsmen and designers at Hamble; these personnel were formed into a small drawing office which, although remaining an Avro unit, was contracted in its entirety to the Cierva Autogiro Company and worked under Cierva's direct control. At the completion of the C19 programme at Hamble the Avro drawing office joined the remainder of the company at Manchester, while the Cierva concern moved to Hanworth; autogyros were by no means a new sight at Hanworth, the Autogiro Flying Club having been established there some time previously.

Cierva machines were widely demonstrated and displayed during the late-1920s and the 1930s, both at home and overseas. In some cases Cierva flew the machines himself, but more usually the task fell to his test and demonstration pilots, A. H. Rawson and Reggie Brie, the latter also writing a book for would-be autogyro pilots.

In the final year before the move to Hanworth Cierva co-operated with the De Havilland Aircraft Company on the design of a two seat cabin autogyro. This machine, designated C24, employed the driven rotor technique for running up prior to take-off and was built by De Havillands at their Stag Lane, Edgware, works in 1931. With the exception of the Cierva rotor system this was a DH design, drawing heavily on the DH80A Puss Moth in the area of the cabin and forward fuselage. Powered by a 120hp Gipsy III and equipped with a tricycle undercariage, the C24 was built in prototype form only and, after modifications to the rotor system and the addition of a dorsal fin, was granted a 'C of A' in April 1932. The

Below: **Cierva C19 MkIII, G-AAYP, seen here after modification to MkIV standard, was flown in the 1932 Skegness Air Race by Reggie Brie who took second place. Note the drive shaft for the rotor starting just ahead of the forward pylon legs.** *Imperial War Museum, via the author*

sole C24, G-ABLM, is today part of the Science Museum's aeronautical collection, but is on loan to the Mosquito Aircraft Museum for exhibition at Salisbury Hall following restoration by Hawker Siddeley apprentices at Hatfield and Leavesden.

Up until 1932 all autogyros suffered from one major drawback in that their aeroplane-type control surfaces were subject to a severe loss of effectiveness at low forward speeds, particularly of course at take-off and in the final seconds before landing. But the Cierva C30, which appeared in that year, incorporated a system of direct control by means of a tilting rotor assembly; the rotor attitude was used to govern the direction of flight totally independently of any moveable control surfaces, the ailerons, elevators and rudder being dispensed with altogether. The tilting rotor system was first tested on a C19 Mk V at Hanworth before the prototype C30 was built by National Flying Services Ltd on behalf of Cierva. In the C30 the attitude of rotor was determined by movement of an inverted control column suspended from the rotor head to the rear of the two cockpits; the C30 was intended to be flown from the rear cockpit, but for training purposes an angled extension piece was attached to the column near the point at which it entered the rotor assembly, thus permitting dual control, the majority of the controls and instruments being duplicated in the front cockpit. The control column was universally hinged on a cross-member between the rear pylon legs and coupled via a ball joint to a rigid lever which was in turn connected to the base of the rotor head, below the lateral and longitudinal hinges — thus when the column was displaced from the neutral position it turned about the universal hinge and pushed the ball in the opposite direction, so causing the rotor to tilt and the machine to move in the direction in which the column had been pushed. This was a considerable advance over all previous autogyros since it made it possible for the pilot to maintain full and positive directional control from take-off until the actual moment of touchdown, irrespective of forward speed. The rotor of the C30 consisted of a three-bladed assembly of 37ft diameter and was mounted atop a tripod pylon immediately above the front cockpit. A large fixed tailplane, with 45° dihedral on the tips and inverted aerofoil section on the port side, was fitted to maintain stability and counteract the torque reaction of the fuselage to the propeller rotation. A steerable tailwheel was provided for manoeuvring on the ground; brakes were fitted to the main wheels, but these did not act differentially and were only intended to prevent forward movement when the engine was running-up prior to take-off, not for steering or arresting forward motion during taxying or after landing.

This design went into production as the C30A, with a four-legged pylon, folding rotor blades for ease of hangarage, and a modified undercarriage with wider

Below: **The Westland CL20, designed by G. Lepere, was developed in 1934-35 but only flew in prototype form. Development was cut short owing to Cierva's commitment to other projects.** *Courtesy Westland Helicopters Ltd.*

track and additional radius rods, becoming the first practical stall-free aircraft to reach production status. The tilting rotor system of control made the C30A highly manoeuvrable and, by comparison with earlier machines, easy to fly, the aircraft automatically assuming the correct angle of bank for any rate of turn induced by displacement of the rotor and positive control being maintained at all stages of flight. Mechanical starting by the auxiliary power take off method previously described was employed. Production in the UK was undertaken by the Avro Co at Manchester which built a total of 77 machines; of these, 37 went to UK civil users, 28 were exported, and 12 were supplied to the RAF under the designation Avro 671 Rota I. The powerplant was the 140hp Armstrong Siddeley Genet Major 1A, known as the 'Civet' in RAF service. Avro-built C30As were subjected to military trials and evaluation in Belgium, Denmark, France, Jugoslavia, Russia and Spain. Overseas production was undertaken by Focke-Wulf, which built 40 using a Seimens engine, and Liore et Olivier, which used the 175hp Salmson 9NE on the 25 machines that they built under the designation LeO 301.

Many C30As went to flying clubs and schools as well as to private individuals, but some did see more workmanlike service as aerial photographic platforms, communications aircraft in remote and inaccessible areas, and as airborne observation posts for traffic control, etc. Probably the leading commercial exponent of the type was the Swede Rolf von Bahr; von Bahr was managing director of the Swedish company Helikopter-Flyg, having gained his 'B' licence in England in 1934, and was for many years the only autogyro pilot in Sweden. He found the C30A ideal for operations in his native country and at the outbreak of war in 1939 he placed himself and his machines at the disposal of the Naval authorities in the Oeresund district of southern Sweden. The war years were spent flying reconnaissance patrols over the waters of the Skagerrak and the southern part of the Baltic Sea, each patrol lasting around two hours and being carried out in temperatures as low as $-15°C$, a daunting prospect in an open cockpit with nothing but a cold and cruel sea below. Von Bahr's activities were of inestimable value to Swedish shipping, and ranged from the plotting, reporting,

Right: Avro-built and German-registered C30A, D-EKOP, showing the four-legged pylon and wide track undercarriage adopted for the production models. Flight, *via the author*

and frequently disarming, of mines which were drifting towards Swedish waters, to the ferrying of provisions and medical supplies to ships trapped and frozen fast in the iced-up Baltic during the hard winter months; these missions were made possible by the then unique capability of the autogyro to remain airborne at speeds as low as 15mph, and to remain stationary relative to the ground when headed into even a slight wind. Rescue missions were undertaken on many occasions, making use of the C30A's remarkable take-off and landing distances of about 30yd and 3yd respectively, partially submerged ice floes becoming temporary landing strips to facilitate the collection of a casualty or the delivery of urgently-needed supplies to ships. During the particularly hard winters of 1940 and 1941 von Bahr was kept busy flying relief missions to isolated military installations and civilian communities cut-off by deep snowdrifts, in addition to maintaining his schedule of regular maritime patrols. By 1947 Rolf von Bahr had amassed an incredible total of over 7,000 flying hours on autogyros, a figure which few pilots, if any, could match, and miraculously survived two ditchings in the inhospitable waters of the Baltic.

By the time the C30A entered quantity production in 1934 the Cierva Autogiro Co was already well-advanced in development work on the next major innovation in autogyro design, the 'Autodynamic' rotor head, which allowed true vertical take-offs to be made by a technique known as 'jump starting'. This technique, perfected in 1936 following trial installations in the C30 prototype, G-ACFI, and the C30A, G-ACWF, involved over-speeding the rotor assembly with the blades set at zero incidence; once the rotor speed was high enough the drive clutch was disengaged and the blades placed in positive pitch, the resulting lift causing the machine to jump to a height of some 20ft, whereupon it commenced forward flight under the influence of the propeller, the rotor continuing to revolve in autorotation. Severe vibration problems were encountered in the Autodynamic head, but these had been overcome by the time the jump-start technique was applied to a production model; this was the C40, a side-by-side two seater powered by a Salmson 9NG engine of 175hp. Despite the modified cockpit arrangement, a new extended undercarriage, and modifications to the tail unit, including the re-introduction of a rudder, the C40 retained the general appearance of the C30A. Production was by Oddie, Bradbury, and Cull Ltd at Eastleigh, final assembly being undertaken by the British Aircraft Manufacturing Co at Hanworth, but only nine examples were built.

Several factors combined to cause the ultimate demise of the autogyro. Foremost among them was

Above: **Rota K4232 seen postwar while operating with Helicopter-Flyg as SE-AZB. Note that a rudder has been added in lieu of the normal trim tab.** *Rolf von Bahr, via J. M. Bruce*

the untimely death of Juan de la Cierva in the crash of a KLM DC-2 airliner at Croydon in December 1936, which robbed the autogyro industry of its leading exponent and innovator, a loss from which it never fully recovered; it is ironic in the extreme that Cierva, who had carried out much of his own early test and development flying, at considerable risk to life and limb, should have met his end in an accident while travelling as a passenger on a scheduled airline service. The second factor was really a combination of economic realities; by comparison with contemporary fixed-wing aircraft the autogyro was expensive to purchase, more costly to operate and maintain, and suffered from the high noise levels and exposure to the elements associated with its open cockpit. If Cierva's life had been prolonged, it is probable that he would have turned his attention to redressing the situation and making the autogyro more competitive, having by 1936 reached a point where the machine's technical performance could be considered satisfactory and time might be devoted to making its operation more economical and comfortable. But Cierva did not live, and by the late-1930s the autogyro's popularity was firmly on the wane, many of the original machines having been either sold abroad or placed in long-term storage at Hanworth; 13 of the civil C30As, however, were given a new lease of life when they were impressed into the RAF in the early years of World War 2 to serve alongside the surviving Avro Rotas.

During the war, research to develop a practical helicopter continued apace and began to bear fruit. By the end of 1941 Igor Sikorski had developed his VS-300 design to the point where, in addition to satisfying the strict performance criteria for classification as a helicopter, it could carry a sufficient payload to enable it to perform a useful load-carrying function. Thus the VS-300 was the world's first practical helicopter, a functional machine rather than just another stage in the research and development programme; the helicopter, that elusive means of transport foreseen by such visionaries as Archimedes, Leonardo da Vinci, and Jules Verne, had finally arrived, and in its coming had removed any lingering doubts as to the fate of the autogyro. After the war the helicopter continued to make steady progress, due largely to its obvious military potential which ensured that funds for development were readily made available by interested governments, while the autogyro was almost totally ignored. Militarily obsolete, the remaining RAF Rotas and C30As were put up for disposal, most passing into private ownership; three went to Helikopter-Flyg in Sweden, while another three were bought by Fairey Aviation to enable them to gain rotary wing experience in

connection with their first helicopter design, the Gyrodyne. The vast majority had been withdrawn from use by 1950, although a few isolated examples remained active until 1957-58 before succumbing.

Interest in the autogyro began to revive somewhat in the late-1950s due mainly to the work of Igor Bensen in the USA and Wg Cdr Ken Wallis in the UK, both of whom have devoted much time and effort to the development of small single and two-seat machines, showing that these can be a safe and economical mode of transport for both business and pleasure. The tasks successfully accomplished by these diminutive aircraft inlude aerial photography and surveillance, light agricultural duties, radar calibration, and a host of other jobs, many of which have been carried out in circumstances and conditions which precluded the use of conventional aircraft or helicopters. However, the autogyro's main use today is for sport and pleasure flying and it seems unlikely that we shall see it in widespread use in any other role in the foreseeable future.

British military interest in autogyros dates back to 1925 when the Air Ministry's then Director of Scientific Research, Maj H. E. Wimperis, invited Juan de la Cierva to bring his C6A to Farnborough and demonstrate it before an audience of Ministry officials. The invitation was accepted and the demonstration took place on 10 October that year, with F. T. Courtney at the controls, and resulted in the Ministry placing an order for two modified

machines, a C6C which flew as J8068 and a C6D which was civil registered as G-EBTW, both of which were delivered the following year. The C6C was written-off in an accident in 1927 due to fatigue failure at the blade roots, and G-EBTW was modified to the instructions of the Air Ministry as a C8R and given the military serial J8930. The Air Ministry, through the RAE at Farnborough, maintained an active interest in rotary-winged flight and a variety of machines were subjected to research and evaluation programmes at RAE; in the main these were Cierva types, but at one point the Ministry hedged its bets somewhat by giving Saunders-Roe a contract to supply one example of the Heliogyre, a patented Isacco design which incorporated a tip-driven rotor.

One noteworthy design supported by the Air Ministry was the Westland-built Cierva C29, a five seater powered by a 600hp Armstrong Siddeley Panther engine and with a 50ft diameter rotor. With a projected top speed of 160mph and enclosed cabin accommodation for four passengers besides the pilot, the C29 was envisaged as an air taxi, providing fast transport from city centre to city centre independent of large and costly airports. However, the C29 was plagued from the outset with ground resonance problems and, despite attempts to maintain rotor balance, the vibration persisted and the project was abandoned, thus halting progress on an idea which was several decades ahead of its time.

Following some eight years of research and evaluation of various types at RAE the Air Ministry placed a contract with the Cierva Autogiro Company in 1933 for the supply of ten C30As, the machines to be built by Avro at their Manchester works under the designation Avro 671 Rota I. These aircraft were intended for communications and spotting duties in the Army co-operation role with the Air Defence of

Great Britain, coming under the control of Fighter Command with the RAF re-organisation of July 1936, and AM Spec 16/35 was drawn-up retrospectively around this application.

The first Rota, K4230, was modified by Ciervas at Hanworth to facilitate deck landing operations, and the aircraft was embarked in HMS *Courageous* for trials during the carrier's 1935 summer cruise. The remaining nine aircraft were delivered to the RAF's School of Army Co-operation at Old Sarum in two batches during April and August 1934. Apart from their primary role consideration was also given to the Rota's employment on air-sea rescue duties, and to this end an 11th machine was built by Avro and fitted with floats by Shorts at Rochester; this aircraft was

Top: Rota K4230 carried out deck landing trials on board HMS *Courageous* in 1935.
Imperial War Museum, via the author

Above: K4232, the Rota acquired for the RAF Museum, seen being made ready for flight at Old Sarum in 1935.
RAF Museum, Charles E. Brown collection

delivered to the Marine Aircraft Experimental Establishment at Felixstowe for evaluation in May 1935. Another single example was delivered to the RAE in May 1935 and was engaged on blade flexing tests at RAE and A&AEE, bringing to twelve the total number of Rotas supplied to the AM.

The Rota's pre-war career was relatively short-lived; two aircraft were lost in flying accidents, one was grounded as an instructional airframe, and a fourth was scrapped at the completion of the research programme on which it had been engaged. The remaining eight were withdrawn from use during the second half of 1938 and placed in storage at No 26 MU. By the early part of World War 2 only three of the original 12 Rotas were still on charge and these, together with 13 impressed civil C30As, were assigned to the task of calibration flying in support of the Chain Home and Chain Home Low coastal radar stations.

The original unit concerned with calibration duties was No 5 Radio Servicing Section, based at Duxford. No 5 RSS, which was re-named No 74 (Signals) Wing in February 1941, flew an assortment of light aircraft types, mainly impressed civil machines. The autogyro section of the Wing broke away in February 1942 to form No 1448 (Radar Calibration) Flight, moving to

Halton the following month. In mid-1943 the unit was again re-named, then becoming No 529 (RC) Squadron, but remained at Halton until August 1944 when it moved to its final home at Crazies Hill, near Henley-on-Thames. The autogyros operated for most of the time on individual detachment, flying from airfields close to the radar station to which they were assigned for calibration duties. Fighter escorts were provided by the RAF or Fleet Air Arm whenever the machines were operating in an area where enemy aircraft might be encountered; although no autogyro was lost to enemy action several did come under fire but were saved by their own agility and the rapid intervention of their escorting fighter.

An order had been placed in 1937 for a batch of seven Cierva C40s, envisaged as replacements for the Rotas; two of these aircraft were diverted for civil use, probably by Ciervas, before delivery, the remaining five being delivered in the first half of 1939. Replacements for the two diverted machines were supplied later the same year. The C40s were employed on various tasks, including research work at RAE, communications duties at Fighter and Coastal Command HQs, and the training of rotary-wing pilots with the Autogyro Training Flight (ATF),

Below: **Impressed C30A AP507, formerly G-ACWP, seen while serving with No 1448 (RC) Flight.** *Imperial War Museum, via the author*

in addition to augmenting the Rotas and C30As with the calibration units. The restricted production of the C40 made it extremely vulnerable to shortage of spares; two aircraft were scrapped due to non-availability of essential spares and by the end of 1944 the type had been withdrawn completely.

The ATF, formed at Odiham in April 1940, provided fixed-wing pilots with rotary-wing conversion training using a mixture of C30As and C40s.

Seven Warner Scarab-engined Pitcairn machines were bought by direct purchase from the manufacturer in 1941, but three of the batch were lost at sea during the delivery voyage across the North Atlantic in January of 1942. The four survivors went into service with A&AEE and No 74 (Signals) Wing, but all had been wrecked in flying accidents or otherwise written off by the end of the following year.

Below: **Another view of K4232 in Sweden as SE-AZB with, it is believed, Rolf von Bahr in the cockpit.** *Rolf von Bahr, via J. M. Bruce*

The Rotas and C30As continued to serve with the calibration unit throughout the war, No 529 (RC) Squadron being the RAF's first and only operational autogyro squadron. Unfortunately from our point of view the activities of the calibration unit were, of necessity, carried out under conditions of the very strictest secrecy and the contribution of these aircraft and crews to the operational efficiency of Britain's wartime radar network can only be guessed at, considerable though it must have been. In early-1945 the Squadron received a single example of the Sikorsky R-4 helicopter, known as the Hoverfly I in RAF service; the Helicopter Training Flight had been formed at Andover at the beginning of the year, and the Hoverfly employed by No 529 (RC) Squadron represented the first use of a helicopter by an operational RAF squadron, providing a foretaste of what was to come in later years. The Squadron was disbanded in October 1945, the Rotas and C30As being flown to No 5 MU for disposal; all passed into civil ownership though not all returned to active flying.

By way of a postscript to British military involvement with autogyros the Army Air Corps subjected three one-man machines to trials and evaluation at the AAC Centre at Middle Wallop in 1962-63. These machines were WA-116s, designed by Wg-Cdr Ken Wallis and built by the Beagle Aircraft Company at Shoreham. After evaluation all three aircraft were returned to Beagle, and no order was placed.

One of the Rotas which did return to active flying after withdrawal from RAF service was K4232, which was sold to Rolf von Bahr's company Helikopter-Flyg and appeared on the Swedish register as SE-AZB. It is this aircraft which was recovered from Sweden in 1979 and, restored to her 1934 condition and markings, was due to go on display at the RAF Museum, Hendon before the end of 1980. Restoration has been carried out by the Museum's staff at Cardington and, as always, has been painstakingly thorough — as much attention has been paid to the interior structure and components as to the exterior. At Hendon the Rota has made a most interesting addition to the aircraft collection, recalling the Air Ministry's 20year involvement with autogyros and the RAF's first employment of rotary-winged aircraft in an operational role, both of which aspects deserve more public recognition than they have received to date.

Acknowledgement
The author wishes to acknowledge the help of the RAF Museum authorities and staff for provision of photographic facilities and access to historical material.

Above: **A view of K4232 following its restoration at Cardington and showing the salient features of the Avro 671 Rota I.**

Right: **Close up view of K4232 showing the restored Genet Major (Civet) engine and Fairey-Reed metal propeller.**
Both R. A. Nicholls

Leading Particulars — Avro 671 Rota I

Engine one 140hp Armstrong Siddeley Genet Major (Civet I)
Maximum AUW 1,900lb
Initial climb rate 700ft/min
Maximum speed 110mph
Maximum range 250 miles
Service ceiling 8,000ft
Overall length 19ft 8½in

Height overall (in level flight) 11ft 2in
Tail span 10ft 2in
Diameter of rotor disc 37ft 00in
Rotor blade incidence 2°40′
Range of rotor hub movement Forward 2½°, Aft 7½°, Port 3°, Starboard 5°
Propeller diameter 7ft 00in
Undercarriage track 9ft 5in

Autogyros in UK Military Service

Serial	Type	TOC	SOC	Remarks
J8068	Cierva C6C (Avro 574)	1926	1927	Avro-built. W/o 1927
J8930	Cierva C8R (Avro 587)	1927	n.d.	Avro-built. Modified from C6D, G-EBTW
J8931	Cierva C8L/I (Avro 586)	1927	n.d.	Avro-built
J9038	Parnall Gyroplane	1928	n.d.	Parnall-built Cierva C10
K1171	Isacco Heliogyre	6.1.30	30.12.31	Used on research at RAE
K1696	Cierva C19/II (Avro 620)	6.11.30	21.2.31	Avro-built. Formerly G-AAYO
K1948	Cierva C19/II (Avro 620)	16.1.31	14.3.34	C/n 5142. Avro-built. Formerly G-ABCM
K3663	Cierva C29	n.d.	26.6.39	AS Panther II engine
K4230	Avro 671 Rota I	23.6.34	6.3.39	Deck landing trials, 1935
K4231	Avro 671 Rota I	23.6.34	5.11.36	Crashed, 9.9.36 — damaged beyond repair
K4232	Avro 671 Rota I	23.6.34	21.5.46	Sold to Helikopter-Flyg after SOC — to Swedish register as SE-AZB
K4233	Avro 671 Rota I	23.6.34	4.5.46	Sold to Southern Aircraft (Gatwick) after SOC — became G-AHUC before sale in Sweden
K4234	Avro 671 Rota I	23.6.34	5.3.35	Crashed, 21.1.35 — damaged beyond repair
K4235	Avro 671 Rota I	29.8.34	23.5.46	Sold to Fairey Aviation after SOC — reg. G-AHMJ. Currently preserved, Shuttleworth Collection
K4236	Avro 671 Rota I	29.8.34	15.10.36	RTS at Martlesham Heath
K4237	Avro 671 Rota I	29.8.34	NEA 1938	To No 3 SOTT as 1142M on 14.10.38
K4238	Avro 671 Rota I	29.8.34	6.3.39	
K4239	Avro 671 Rota I	29.8.34	1.8.46	Sold to private owner after SOC — to civil register as G-AIOC
K4296	Avro 671 Rota I	14.5.35	30.11.38	Float-equipped by Shorts at Rochester — evaluated MAEE, Felixstowe
K4775	Avro 671 Rota I	3.1.35	5.11.37	To contract no 354064/34 for research use at RAE and A&AEE

Serial	Type	TOC	SOC	Remarks
K6553	Cierva Gyroplane	n.a.	n.a.	Cancelled order — serials
K6554				reserved but not taken up
L7589	Cierva C40	23.1.39	14.6.40	7 aircraft to AM Spec 2/36
L7590	Cierva C40	21.1.39	5.10.41	SOC due to non-availability of spares
L7591	Cierva C40	5.5.39	29.6.42	Believed RTS by Cunliffe-Owen
L7592	Cierva C40	n.a.	n.a.	Diverted to civil use before
L7593				delivery. Serials not taken up
L7594	Cierva C40	5.5.39	7.9.44	SOC as obsolete
L7595	Cierva C40	5.5.39	5.10.41	RTS following flying accident on 18.1.41
P9636	Cierva C40	?.?.39	7.9.44	SOC as obsolete
T1419	Cierva C40	19.12.39	n.d.	To contract 968954/38
V1186	Cierva C30A	12.12.39	30.11.43	C/n 731. Impressed, ex G-ACWR. Crashed into sea off Worthing, 24.10.43 — recovered but not repairable
V1187	Cierva C30A	12.12.39	9.5.46	C/n 717. Impressed, ex G-ACWO. Sold to Southern Aircraft (Gatwick) after SOC, but not RTR
AP506	Cierva C30A	1.6.40	24.5.46	C/n 715. Impressed ex G-ACWM. RTR as G-ACWM after SOC
AP507	Cierva C30A	1.6.40	n.d.	C/n 728. Impressed, ex G-ACWP. Preserved, Science Museum
AP508	Cierva C30A	1.6.40	8.10.41	C/n 712. Impressed, ex PH-HHH. Crashed into sea off Seaton, Devon, 16.4.41
AP509	Cierva C30A	1.6.40	17.5.46	C/n 732. Impressed, ex G-ACWS. Sold to CAC after SOC, and RTR as G-AHUC, later SE-AZA
AP510	Cierva C30A	2.6.40	6.6.46	C/n 775. Impressed, ex G-ACYE. Sold to private owner after SOC and RTR as G-ACYE
BV999	Cierva C30A	9.1.41	23.4.46	C/n 737. Impressed, ex G-ACXW. Sold to Fairey Aviation after SOC, and RTR as G-ACXW
BW828	Pitcairn PA-39	n.a.	n.a.	Lost at sea during delivery ex
BW829	Pitcairn PA-39	n.a.	n.a.	USA. Direct purchase from
BW830	Pitcairn PA-39	n.a.	n.a.	Pitcairn Co. Contract A/5012
BW831	Pitcairn PA-39	n.d.	n.d.	
BW832	Pitcairn PA-39	n.d.	n.d.	
BW833	Pitcairn PA-39	?.?.41	19.11.42	SOC after flying acident
BW834	Pitcairn PA-39	?.?.41	?.7.42	RTS by Cunliffe-Owen
DG670	Hafner ARIII Gyroplane	28.4.41	11.4.42	Impressed for RAE use, ex G-ADMV. RTS at 40 MU, Oxford

Serial	Type	TOC	SOC	Remarks
DR622 *	Cierva C30A	1.6.41	?.4.46	C/n 771. Impressed, ex G-ACYH. Sold to private owner after SOC, and RTR as G-AHRP
DR623 *	Cierva C30A	1.6.41	23.4.46	C/n 710. Impressed, ex G-ACWH. Sold to CAC after SOC, and RTR as G-AHLE
DR624 *	Cierva C30A	1.6.41	23.4.46	C/n 708. Impressed, ex G-ACWF. Sold to Fairey Aviation after SOC, and RTR as G-AHMI
HM580 *	Cierva C30A	2.9.42	23.5.46	C/n 726. Impressed, ex G-ACUU. Sold to CAC after SOC, and RTR as G-AIXE, later reverted to G-ACUU. Preserved, Duxford
HM581 *	Cierva C30A	2.9.42	13.5.46	C/n 705. Impressed, ex G-ACUI. Sold to Essex Aero Ltd after SOC, and RTR as G-AHTZ
XR942	Beagle-Wallis WA-116	n.a.	n.a.	C/n B201. W/o at Shoreham before delivery. Serial transferred to c/n B202
XR942	Beagle-Wallis WA-116	?.?.62	?.?.63	C/n B202. Civil registered G-ARZA before and after AAC trials at Middle Wallop
XR943	Beagle-Wallis WA-116	?.?.62	?.?.63	C/n B203. Civil registered G-ARZB before and after AAC trials at Middle Wallop
XR944	Beagle-Wallis WA-116	?.?.62	?.?.63	C/n B204. Civil registered G-ASDY after AAC trials at Middle Wallop

Note Aircraft marked thus * were rebuilt at Duxford from dismantled group assemblies during 1941-42.

Abbreviations

AAC=Army Air Corps
A&AEE=Aeroplane & Armament Experimental Establishment
AS=Armstrong Siddeley
CAC=Cierva Autogiro Co Ltd
C/n=Constructor's number
MAEE=Marine Aircraft Experimental Establishment
n.a.=not applicable
n.d.=no details
NEA=Non-Effective Aircraft List
RAE=Royal Aircraft Establishment
RTR=restored to register (civil)
RTS=reduced to spares
SOTT=School of Technical Training

SOC=Struck Off Charge
TOC=Taken On Charge
W/o=written-off

Above: The first of the RAF's Hercules to be 'stretched' to the new CMk3 configuration, XV223, seen at Lockheed-Georgia Company's Marietta, Ga plant after conversion in late-1979, and alongside a standard length CMk1, XV217. Clues to the location of the fuselage plugs on '223' are provided by comparing the distances between the aft blade aerial and dorsal fin extension and between the forward cabin window and RAF titles. *Lockheed-Georgia*

Stretching the RAF's
HERCULES

AMID ALL the talk about the declining number of aircraft in the RAF's fixed wing air transport force (ATF) a less publicised development has been the capacity improvement stemming from a novel modification programme involving 30 of the Service's Lockheed Hercules. Providing an exception for the first time to the previously standard size of the military versions of the Hercules, a batch of the RAF's fleet of C-130Ks is being stretched by 15ft in fuselage length to assume the dimension of the commercial, L-100-30 variant. This programme will add the equivalent of up to 10 new C-130s to the ATF without the additional costs of extra crews, ground support or spares that would have arisen from the procurement of a like number of new aircraft. The stretched Hercules C Mk3s, as they are designated in RAF service, can carry 128 troops or seven cargo pallets instead of the original C Mk1's payload of 92 troops or five cargo pallets.

Right: **The RAF's first Hercules CMk3 makes a commemorative flypast at Marietta, Ga in company with a CMk1 before returning to the UK.** *Lockheed-Georgia Co.*

Left: **Following the first 'Super Hercules' conversion carried out by the manufacturer, the remaining 29 aircraft in the programme are being modified by Marshall of Cambridge (Engineering), the authorised C-130 Hercules service centre in the UK. Here a front fuselage plug, 100 inches in depth, is being positioned for connection to the nose section and centre fuselage on XV219; the connection involves the use of 688 bolts, mainly ¼in size.**

Below: **In the foreground are the two plugs for a Hercules fuselage stretch, rear plug on the left and front plug on the right. In the left background, XV219 can be seen awaiting connection of its tail section to the centre fuselage-mounted rear plug.** *Crown Copyright, Ministry of Defence*

Above: **A new rear plug (lighter shaded ring) seen on XV219 before reconnection of the tail section. The rear plug is 80 inches long and is fastened with a total of 522 bolts, again mainly of ¼in size.**

Left: **Hercules XV219 with front and rear plugs aligned and attachd to the aircraft respectively.**
Crown Copyright, Ministry of Defence

Above: **Having been stretched to the CMk3 length, XV207 is seen in the final stages of completion at Marshalls before its redelivery to RAF Lyneham, Wilts.**
Crown Copyright, Ministry of Defence

Wardair-

Above: A commemorative portrait of the aircraft at either end of Wardair's history to date – the restored Fox Moth, CF-DJB, parked alongside the Boeing 747-124, C-FFUN *Romeo Vachon,* at Toronto on 8 November 1978.
Caz Caswell/Flightlines International

a dream, now reality

DAVID H. KIRKMAN *Flightlines International*

THE HISTORY of Wardair is really the story of one man — founder, creator and president of the most successful independent charter airline in Canada, Maxwell William Ward. Born in Edmonton on 22 November 1921, Max Ward joined the Royal Canadian Air Force in 1940 and started out on the courses leading to the award of his wings. In 1941 he went to High River, Alberta flying Tiger Moths and then on to Claresholme where they had Cessna T50s. In a class of 64 he graduated with top marks and seemed certain to go abroad to fly Hurricanes; but to his dismay he was chosen, along with one other member of the course, to train as a flying instructor at Trenton. He took his Instructors Rating and was posted to Monckton, New Brunswick.

He wanted to go overseas very badly and tried everything to make it possible. It is said that he even insulted the Chief Instructor, but this only made them

more determined to keep him from going. At least he was flying and that was what he wanted to do. He was discharged from the RCAF in 1945, at the age of 24.

With plenty of prospecting going on in the Northwest Territories Max Ward knew he could obtain a job as a bush pilot, there being not too many airline pilots around at this time. Max started up in Edmonton in 1945 flying a war asset Cessna T50 with Jack Moare. But the business did not go too well and Max decided that before being made redundant, he would leave with the idea of going to Yellowknife where there was a great demand for pilots with their own aircraft. And so, in 1946, Max Ward formed his first company — Polaris Charter — based at Yellowknife. The major problem of course was to buy an aeroplane.

He was fortunate to have saved $1,500 from his War Bonds and decided to travel to Toronto to see

44

Phil Garrett at de Havillands. He was unable to see Phil, but all the same put a deposit on a Fox Moth with floats, wheels and skis at a cost of $10,500. The registration was CF-DJC, later to be used on Wardair's first Boeing 747, named *Phil Garrett*. With the help of a friend of the family, Ward boosted his deposit to $2,500 and arrived at Yellowknife with no operating licence to run an airline — just a plan.

The one-man outfit was a return to the true spirit of flying. The pilot. Max Ward, was seated in an open cockpit while the passengers (or cargo) remained in the relative comfort of the cabin below. Gold prospecting was booming but the flying was arduous — virtually non-stop from dawn to dusk. Wrapping the engine of the Fox Moth in canvas overnight to ensure its starting in the morning and landing in remote areas to brew tea over a bush fire and keep warm, are not the easiest procedures to support the formative days of a new airline.

On one occasion in 1946, not long after taking delivery of 'JC, Max flew two prospectors to a small lake whereupon one of them assisted in pushing the Fox Moth back from the dock. It was windy and ice was beginning to form, and when the willing helper got clear his coat caught a catch on the oil tank which flipped open the oil drain. The aircraft took-off without any problem but soon started to run rough, the oil pressure dropped and finally the engine died. Max landed the Moth on Lake Arsenault and

skimmed over the ice into the open water in the bay. He moved the craft up to the shoreline and checked for damage — the bearings were gone. So there he was marooned in the North, which was freezing up fast, with no engine and no idea of how to obtain help. Then came the recollection that there was a camp over on the next lake where the water was deeper and thus would not freeze up so quickly. On foot he set out and when just approaching the lake saw a Norseman taking off. Waiting until the aircraft was nearer, he fired his Very Pistol toward it; the pilot turned out to be another famous bush pilot by the name of Ernie Botha. They both returned to Yellowknife in one piece.

Max did not have much money but relayed his tale to Punch Dickens at de Havilland (whose name was later to be carried on Boeing 707, C-FFAN, and then DC-10, C-GXRB) who sent him out a new engine on the helpful basis of no deposit and pay for it later — a problem in itself to sort out. Uiscan Engineering helped in flying the engine out to Arsenault Lake, together with a set of skis. Max lived in the camp of a

Below: **The Stinson Station Wagon, CF-KJL, owned by Max Ward's partner in Yellowknife Airways, George Pigeon.**
Wardair

Left: **The Bellanca Skyrocket, CF-EQP, docked on the river at Fort Nelson, BC in 1948 with Max Ward repairing an oil leak. The aircraft carried the title and colours of Yellowknife Airways.**

Below: **Wardair's headquarters in 1953 – the office is on the right and the shop on the left. The aircraft at the pier is a Fairchild F11 Husky.**

Bottom right: **Formation of three Wardair Otters –CF-ITF, IFP and GBY, all fitted with skis – over the Northwest Territories in 1955.** *Wardair*

mining company and walked five miles every day to the Moth's location in temperatures as low as 50° below zero. He changed the floats to skis and worked on the engine — his first engine change. Ten days later saw him pushing it back for the lake.

Then in 1947 the early period of the pioneer flyer's solo operations was modified by the interest of the Air Transport Board. Romeo Vachon of the ATB came to Yellowknife and saw that Max had Polaris Air Charter painted on the side of the Moth; owing to the regulations a licence should not have been issued as the company was too small to be eligible. The only way over this hurdle was to enter into a partnership, which Max promptly did with a fellow aviator named George Pigeon. At first this arrangement worked well; George had a Stinson Station Wagon, CF-KJL, and Yellowknife Airways Ltd was borne. Max borrowed a further $5,000 to put down on a Bellanca Skyrocket which also came with floats, wheels and skis. Unfortunately the partnership shortly suffered the loss of the Moth — a hired pilot had taken two passengers up North one January morning and did not return. It appeared that he ran out of oil, panicked and crashed (quite by chance, the aircraft was found later). Within twelve months, therefore, Max Ward was without an aircraft and the partnership was breaking up due to personal reasons. On top of this there were debts of around $2,000. Clearly it was time to quit bush flying for a while and although Max Ward continued as a hired pilot for Associated Airways, in 1949 he travelled to Lethbridge, Alberta and there worked on construction sites as an apprentice, saving cash as hard as he could with the intent of starting again.

By 1952, all debts repaid and with an operating plan for a new company to be known as Wardair, Max Ward's hopes were alive once more. A second visit was made to de Havilland to purchase a $96,000 DHC-3 Otter and with further loans secured, he was successful in obtaining the last of the hand-built

machines, c/n 5, CF-GBY. However, a further ten months were to elapse before the Air Transport Board granted a licence for the operation of the aircraft, to take effect from 6 June 1953.

Thus it was 1953 which saw the start of what was to become the largest charter airline in Canada. The Otter operated on floats in the summer and skis during the winter months, and in the following years Wardair were to use a total of five single-engined Otters, all painted in the distinctive colour scheme of blue trimmed with red and with white outlines. Wardair steadily expanded, with another DHC-3 Otter purchased in 1954. De Havilland products had proved well for Max and so it was no surprise to see another DHC product added to the fleet in 1956, the DHC-2 Beaver, CF-HNN. By now the payroll had risen to 13 people.

The purchase of Wardair's first heavy type, a Bristol 170 Freighter bought from Trans Canada Airlines came in 1957. It was modified by replacing its mainwheels with those from a C-130 Hercules so as to double its 'footprint' and allow it to operate from unprepared strips. The Bristol became the workhorse of the fleet; a further four examples were purchased and were ferried from Weston-super-Mare in the UK in 1967. Capable of lifting six tons of freight or 44 passengers, the Freighters did much to open up the Canadian North, landing on frozen lakes to supply developing mines and transporting building materials and fuel to remote parts of the Arctic islands. During the summers of 1959 and 1960 a Supermarine Stranraer, CF-BXO, was used for northern freighting operations. This is the aircraft now preserved at the Royal Air Force Museum, Hendon; it was also operated by Pacific Western and Trans Canada Airlines.

Wardair's northern operations continued to expand to the extent that a DC-6A/B was lease-purchased from Canadian Pacific and put to work in the late-winter and spring of 1961/62. At that time of the year the days are the longest and the ice covering over the lakes is at its thickest. During the summer, however, the aircraft was idle for much of the time and Max Ward made the decision which was later to prove Wardair's success. He converted the aircraft cabin to a 91-seat passenger layout and flew his first charter flight over the North Pole to Europe. With a refuelling stop in Greenland, the trip took over 19hr and involved destinations in England, Denmark and Norway. Nine flights were run with a total passenger count of 712 representing 2% of all trans-Atlantic

Top: **The DC-6B leased from Canadian Pacific seen at Edmonton in 1962 — this aircraft paved the way for Wardair charters across the North Atlantic.** *Wardair*

Above: **A Beaver being unloaded from Bristol 170, CF-TFX, at DHC's Downsview plant.**
De Havilland Canada

non-scheduled traffic in 1962. But the effort was not good enough. Although the average load factor of 87% was satisfactory, most of the company's money was lost on the venture — a massive $370,000. The lease-purchased DC-6 was promptly repossessed by Canadian Pacific and Max sought a more favourable agreement elsewhere with a similar aircraft.

The outcome was a 3-year conditional sales agreement on a DC-6B from KLM at a cost of $300,000. The previous deal had involved five times that figure. The following year saw Wardair on the Atlantic run once more with an almost 100% load factor. In 38 flights a total 3,432 passengers were carried and in 1964 the first profit out of the overseas charter business was realised. Wardair was building a healthy reputation with 52 flights in 1964 (4,285 passengers) and 71 in 1965 (5,822).

Northern operations continued all the while and re-equipment commenced in 1963 with DHC-6 Twin Otters replacing the Otters and Beavers. The DC-6 flights had opened up additional business almost by virtue of the overseas gamble and Wardair's experience of over-the-Pole flights became acknowledged as a valued asset. When the Government decided to survey the Canadian North, Wardair was among the airlines chosen for the task. On one occasion the DC-6 was equipped by Dominion Observatories with a specially designed magnetometer. The aircraft operated for 17 days, averaging 13hr/day and over 2.5 million sq miles were flown with a crew of seven plus five scientific personnel.

The Northern business was thriving and on this form and with the previous few years' experience of the charters to Europe, Wardair made another momentous step forward. Max Ward leased a $5.5 million Boeing 727-100 from Greyhound Leasing and Financial of Canada Ltd from 1 May 1966. This was

the first Boeing jet to be operated by a Canadian airline and the first on the Canadian register. Appropriately it was named after the famous bush pilot, Cy Becker. It was ideal for Wardair's European charters and that year the number of passengers carried across the Atlantic jumped to 12,047, with 18 flights by the DC-6 and 104 by the B727.

In 1967, 125 trans-Atlantic crossings were made, 58 being in the July peak travel month; the highest utilisation for any B727 during a given month. The aircraft suffered only one 40min delay and averaged 16.85hr/day. Wardair had really taken off. The year 1967 was one of considerable change as well of significant accomplishments. The Boeing 727 had beaten all previous records and the sturdy old Bristol 170s continued to ply their trade in the North, but not without note. On 6 May 1967, Bristol Freighter CF-TFX piloted by Captain Don Braun (whose name was later to be applied to the airline's Dash-7 C-GXVF) became the first wheel-equipped aircraft to land at the North Pole. The aircraft was subsequently retired in 1968 and in May 1970 was donated by Max Ward to Bristol Park, Yellowknife, where it stands today as a monument to its historic past and as a tribute to the role of bush aircraft in opening up the Canadian Arctic.

In September 1967 Wardair went public, selling $3.5 million convertible debentures and 350,000 shares at $2.75, giving a total of $4,462,500. Additionally, a loan of $4.2 million from the Industrial Development Bank, along with equity

51

capital, provided the funds for the purchase of a
Boeing 707-320C and two spare Pratt & Whitney
JT3D-7 turbofan engines. Wardair took delivery of
this, their first big jet, in the following year — the
aircraft was registered CF-FAN. 1969 saw the
delivery of a second B707, a -396C originally destined
for Quebecair; this machine was again leased from
Greyhound.

The next couple of years were relatively quiet —
the business growth continued and the trans-Atlantic
charters benefitted from the new equipment. But
then the alarm bells started to ring when Transport
Canada ordered that affinity charters had to stop. It
looked at the time as though Wardair would be one of
the victims of this new legislation, so Max Ward
considered moving in with Air Canada, selling one
third of his airline's shares to the national carrier and
conducting all their charter business for them. In the
event the link-up went unrealised; Air Canada was
unwilling to have Wardair handle all its charter
business and besides, it seemed that the independent
airline was not to be closed after all. Wardair
continued and grew, and the airline industry realised
that the company was there to stay.

The Boeing 727 had been giving sterling service for
seven years when, in 1973, it was bought from
Greyhound Leasing and then promptly sold at a
modest profit to Cruziero of Brazil. Then came a
surprise move when Wardair acquired a Boeing 747-
1D1 and its associated spares and ground support
equipment. The Jumbo, originally ordered by
Universal before its close-down, was previously
delivered to Braniff. The latter, however, could not
justify the operation and soon sold it, much to the
delight of Wardair whose acquisition was another
'first' — the first 747 ordered by a Canadian airline.

A second B747 was quickly added to the fleet in
1974 and took as its registration that formerly used by
the B727. In the train of further growth, Wardair was
re-organised; the corporate name was changed to
Wardair Canada (1975) Ltd and on 10 June that year
Wardair International Ltd was officially established
as the parent company of the airline. International
Vacations (Intervac), a marketing outlet for the
Wardair flights was formed as was a similar operation
to Intervac in the United Kingdom, Wardair (UK)
Ltd. By 1977 the average aircraft utilisation in the
fleet was 11.6hr/day and the traffic was large, with

Left: **Boeing 707-311C, CF-FAN; the aircraft was
sold later to Kuwait.** *Boeing*

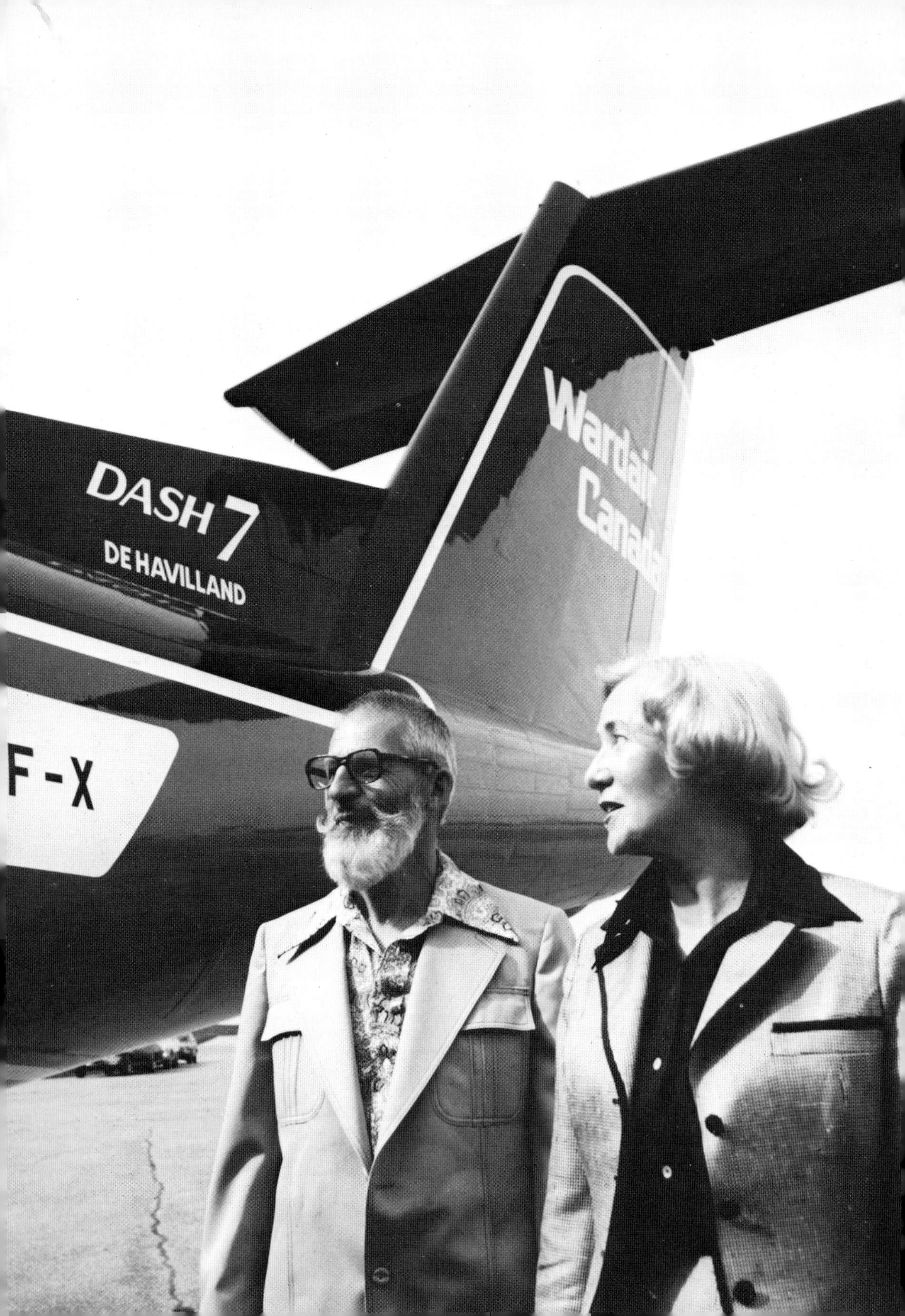
DASH 7
DE HAVILLAND
Wardair
F-X

Above: **The first of the Wardair DC-10 srs 30s to be delivered to the airline, C-GXRC** *W.R. 'Wop' May.* *Caz Caswell/Flightlines International*

Left: **Jean Buck, operations manager of Wardair Northern Operations with former WDA pilot, Don Braun, at the handover ceremony of the first Dash 7 — named after the latter.** *George Hunter*

over two billion passenger miles flown. This was more than double the 1973 figure. An enormous expansion drive took place in 1977 when a new B747 hangar was opened at Edmonton International Airport and orders worth $413 million were placed for two new B747-200Bs and two new DC-10srs30s. The airline's payroll had risen to 1,500, a far cry from the 13 staff employed in 1956.

Wardair was again the first to introduce a new type in Canada when, at a ceremony held at the de Havilland headquarters at Downsview on 23 May 1978, a Dash 7, C-GXVF, was christened *Don Braun.* Mr Braun himself, who made that historic trip in the Bristol 170, was present along with Jean Buck, head of Northern Operations. This was also the first Dash 7 (c/n 7) to be fitted with a cargo door. On 9 June of the same year Wardair's first srs 200 B747 was delivered to Edmonton. This was the start of the most wide-ranging development period in the history of the airline. Once more the aircraft was christened after a famous bush pilot — *Herbert Hollick-Kenyon.*

The four days starting 31 July 1978 marked a very special moment in the airline's annals when it became the only commercial carrier to fly HM Queen Elizabeth II, Prince Philip and Prince Andrew throughout Alberta and Saskatchewan as the royal party visited Canada for the XI Commonwealth Games. Arrangements for the visit started soon after delivery of the Dash 7 in May, the aircraft being chosen on account of its STOL capability. It was assigned 'Royal Flight 712' and a special request was received from Air Cdre A. Winskill of The Queen's Flight that a VIP compartment be made to seat eight. This was duly designed and installed by Wardair's own engineering and maintenance team. In Saskatchewan the Dash 7 was placed under guard until 14.00hrs on July 31, whereupon the crew, W. Pullen — Captain, Dave Watson — First Officer, Brian Whitehead — Flight Engineer, and Flight Attendants Wendy Sutcliff and Mary Anne Rankin, took up their duties for the honoured occasion.

October 1978 saw the Wardair maintenance and purchasing departments relocate their operations from Edmonton to Toronto. This move was caused as the result of several developments, the main one being that Government regulations did not permit Wardair to carry passengers between cities, whilst the bulk of their flights originated from Toronto. Even so, by this time the company served seven Canadian cities: Toronto, Edmonton, Vancouver, Calgary, Winnipeg, Montreal and Ottawa. November and December 1978 saw the departure of the two hard worked Boeing 707s, one to Kuwait, the other to Montana of Austria; and with the arrival of the two new DC-10s Wardair's international fleet became totally wide-bodied. Somewhat of a mix-up in aircraft name dedications occurred when the two DC-10s took up those of the departing B707s. In November, McDonnell Douglas retained the first of the DC-10s, C-GXRB *C. H. Punch Dickens* for flight testing and

Below: **Wardair's first Dash 7, carrying the pre-delivery registration C-GXVF-X and named for Don Braun, seen during a flight test from DHC's Downsview, Ont airfield.** *De Havilland Canada*

instead delivered C-GXRC, *W. R. 'WOP' May*. With the sale of the B707s, C-FFAN the former *C. H. Punch Dickens* went to Kuwait but C-FZYP *W. R. 'WOP' May* was not due to depart until December. Hence two 'WOP Mays' were in operation for a couple of weeks until the 707 left for Austria. On 25 April 1979 the second B747-200 was delivered, arriving at Toronto from Seattle at 18.00hrs. The next day it was officially christened *W. A. 'Doc' Oaks* by the late Doc Oaks' wife Bernice, herself one of Canada's first woman aviators.

Away to the north, Wardair was still operating over the areas covered in its early years. The 23rd of March saw a Dash 7 carry a 30 man scientific team to land on the sea ice at 88°44'N, 175°46'W, just 76 miles from the North Pole. The Department of Energy, Mines and Resources was conducting a two month survey of the Lomonosov Ridge in the Arctic Ocean. On 1 April, an appropriate day, while flying more equipment on this contract, Murrey Oakenfold and Craig Narraway flew over the North Pole at an altitude of 500ft above sea level. Technically, once an aircraft has flown around the Pole it may be considered to have flown around the world. This trip thus became the first non-stop Dash 7 flight around the world, as they circled the North Pole once and headed back south to Alert.

A sad day in world aviation was the 5 June 1979 DC-10 crash of American Airlines' N111AA at Chicago O'Hare Airport. Like many airlines, Wardair was badly hit by the subsequent grounding of the McDonnell Douglas trijet, this causing severe planning difficulties for flight operations and prompting the re-assignment of the B747s so that they more or less flew continuously to transport passengers to their pre-arranged destinations with the minimum of delay. Twenty-five days later, on 30 June, the Canadian Government permitted Wardair to re-commence DC-10 flights and also allowed other operators to resume DC-10 flights in Canadian airspace.

Wardair has been quick off the mark not only in commercial enterprise but also in humanitarian concern as well. On 10 September 1979, the first of many flights were operated on behalf of the Canadian Government to transport Vietnamese refugees. Wardair aircraft are frequently chartered by the Government for such operations, but somehow the company also manages to find the time to execute a little goodwill of its own. Earlier that year, for example, the residents of the tiny island of St Vincent in the Carribean experienced a series of 20 volcanic eruptions leaving many families homeless and without food. On 25 April 1979, ferry flight 151 carried 34,822lb of relief food, clothing, shoes and blankets to Barbados from whence the supplies were transhipped over to St Vincent. All help by Wardair personnel was voluntary, many had stayed to assist beyond long maintenance shifts, while numerous other employees returned from vacation to help with the work.

On 12 February 1980 the Conservative Government announced significant changes to Canadian Transport Commission regulations by an Order-in-Council which expanded the operating authority of charter air carriers, both domestically and internationally. Following up the new opportunity on 19 March Max Ward announced Wardair's entry into the domestic charter market with once-weekly non-stop flights to Vancouver from Toronto, and vice versa, starting on 8 May. This new step has meant that Wardair can face the 1980s with added confidence. After years of fighting the Canadian Transport Commission and continually criticising the Government for its restrictive aviation policy, the company has been able to offer domestic charters. From 27 October to 12 December 1980 the weekly charters between Toronto and Vancouver were due to be increased to four per week, and services to Edmonton and Calgary were to have been added. Moreover, Wardair has now been authorised to carry cargo on its flights; although initially such flights to Europe were restricted, a cargo network structure was formulated towards the third quarter of 1980.

Also during 1980 Wardair announced the construction of a double bay Boeing 747 hangar at Toronto International Airport, along with an overhaul and office complex. Until the completion of the facility, the company leased additional hangar space from Air Canada, this arrangement expiring in November 1980. Wardair's own hangar site is located at the intersection of the 401 highway and Renforth Drive, such that it lies between the highway and runway 23L. It is unique in being the largest clear span rigid frame structure in North America and it is estimated that it will be seen by more than 200,000 people every day — not a bad form of advertising! By the end of 1981 all Wardair personnel will be located on the new site.

So why has Wardair been so successful? Basically, it is the combination of two major assets, one derived from the other. The first is Maxwell Ward himself, the second his foresight to generate a market, work it and thence to expand it to meet the demand that he has created. The trans-Atlantic charter business was a good example. Faced with a DC-6 which was leaching money in payments while not in use, he felt that there could be a market in the ethnic travel business. There were many postwar immigrants who had happily settled in Canada and yet relished the thought of a trip back to Europe every now and then. Their problem was the high cost of scheduled airline fares or the time taken for the train and boat trip. The answer had to be to reduce both the time and the fare. By testing the water with the Canadian Pacific DC-6, Max Ward proved to himself that the market potential was there.

This type of testing period using leased aircraft is quite a hallmark of Wardair and has been used on nearly every route that they now fly. The principle remains today as sound as it ever was as Wardair tries out the domestic market at the beginning of the 1980s.

Maxwell L. Ward has been honoured on numerous occasions. In 1973 a group of Canadian pilots bestowed on him the 'Companion to the Order of Icarus'. On 15 May of the same year he received the Trans-Canada McKee Trophy, one of Canada's most coveted aviation awards. In 1978 he was given an Honourary Life Membership in the Air Transport Association of Canada; and on 30 May 1979, at the Spring Convention of the University of Alberta in Edmonton, Mr Ward received an Honorary Doctorate of Law. And so they continue; again, on 14 September he was the recipient of the Gordon R. McGregor Memorial Trophy for 1979, presented by the Royal Canadian Air Force Association. The trophy was established in 1972 and honours the late President of Air Canada and is awarded annually in recognition of outstanding and meritorious achievement by Canadians in the field of air transportation. And finally, the airline itself; on 10 March 1980 Wardair was rated airline of the year by Calladine & Baldry and Bay Travel, the other nominees being Air Canada and British Airways. Wardair is unique in the charter airline business in using real china and cutlery, and not plastic ware, with the result that at a recent intercontinental catering exhibition held in the United Kingdom, Wardair in-flight meals were awarded first place.

In the history of any developing airline, however, there has to be that saddening moment. This came to Wardair on 19 October 1979 with the closure of Wardair Northern Operations. To quote a telex sent to all bases and released to the press simultaneously:

'Wardair Canada (1975) Ltd will close down its Yellowknife, NWT base of operations after providing 26 years of Northern Canada bush flying services.

Mr Ward stated the demand for bush flying services at Yellowknife has been decreasing over the past few years and can no longer economically support the size of operations provided by Wardair. Unfortunately, we do not foresee demand for bush flying services increasing in Yellowknife during the next few years as the oil pipeline appears stalled and oil companies are now providing much of their own Northern aircraft

services. Mining exploration in Northern Canada has increased but this demand is seasonal and restricted to two or three summer months. Wardair currently operates five 19-passenger de Havilland Twin Otter bush aircraft, one 50-passenger de Havilland Dash 7 aircraft and one 18-passenger Grumman G1 aircraft from its Yellowknife base.

The company currently employs 37 persons, some of whom will be offered transfers to Wardair's International operation. Wardair ordered two of the new de Havilland Dash 7, 50-passenger STOL aircraft but sold one of the machines plus one de Havilland Twin Otter earlier this year.

The fleet of seven bush aircraft plus the Yellowknife assets of the company are being offered for sale. Wardair's Northern operations contributes 1.8 percent to company gross revenues and was marginally profitable during 1978.

The sale of Wardair's Northern bush service will not affect Wardair's International charter operations.

Mr Ward stated that his association with Northern Canada started in Yellowknife in 1946 and he is sad indeed to see his close ties with the North end after all these years'.

Nevertheless, it was not the total end of Wardair's influence in the north. As recently as 1980 a single DHC-3 Otter was purchased from the Royal Canadian Mounted Police in order that the licences could be maintained. Maybe, some day, the company will commence an expansion programme in the area as they find that they generate the market once more.

Wardair was no more than a dream for a young man in 1946 but through sheer tenacity, inspiration and a good deal of business acumen, it has become a reality. Thus on into the 1980s with the next stage in the company's expansion likely to focus on the requirement for a wide-body twin-jet. Wardair has been looking at the relative merits of the Boeing 767 and Airbus A310 to meet its next generation airliner needs and its plans in this direction are a token of the optimism with which it regards the future.

Acknowledgements
The author gratefully acknowledges the assistance, information and photographs supplied by many Wardair staff, in particular by Doreen Rouse — Mr Ward's secretary, Rita Polegri — Superjet News, Danny McNivan — Vice President of Maintenance, George Bell — Vice President of Personnel (Maint), Les Aalders — engineer, The Boeing Aircraft Co, and de Havilland Canada. Also, special thanks are extended to Max Ward for his encouragement and enthusiasm for the project and finally, to Caz Caswell — Buyer, Wardair, whose meticulous compilation of notes made this article possible.

Aircraft operated by Wardair

Regn	c/n	Aircraft	Notes
CF-DJB	c/n 28	Fox Moth	Current
CF-DJC (1)	29	Fox Moth	Crashed north of Yellowknife, 01.48
CF-GBY	5	DHC-3 Otter	To La Range Aviation, Edmonton
CF-IFF		DHC-3 Otter	
CF-IFP	73	DHC-3 Otter	To Silver Pine Airlines, Manitoba
CF-ITF	89	DHC-3 Otter	To La Sarre Airlines, Quebec
CF-JRS	110	DHC-3 Otter	Written off
C-FMPY	324	DHC-3 Otter	Current, ex-RCMP
CF-HNN	618	DHC-2 Beaver	Written off
CF-IFJ	831	DHC-2 Beaver	To La Range Aviation, Edmonton
CF-VOG	35	DHC-6 Twin Otter	To La Range Aviation, Edmonton
CF-WAF	122	DHC-6 Twin Otter	To Northwest Airlines, Edmonton
C-FWAA	238	DHC-6 Twin Otter	To Bannock Aero
C-FWAH	240	DHC-6 Twin Otter	To Bannock Aero
C-FTFX (2)	340	DHC-6 Twin Otter	To Ptarmigan
C-FWAG (2)	343	DHC-6 Twin Otter	
C-FWAB	349	DHC-6 Twin Otter	To Ptarmigan
C-FWAC (2)	350	DHC-6 Twin Otter	
CF-TFX (1)	13137	Bristol Freighter	Preserved as a monument at Yellowknife, NWT.
CF-WAC (1)	13079	Bristol Freighter	To Lambair 11.70
CF-WAD	13253	Bristol Freighter	Written off, Hay River
CF-WAE	13219	Bristol Freighter	To Norcanair, Prince Rupert, 03.70
CF-WAG (1)	13249	Bristol Freighter	Fell through ice on Great Slave Lake, Snowdrift, NWT 03.05.70. Stripped and sunk.
C-FCOL	64	Gulfstream I	Sold in US
C-GWID	557	MU-2B-35	Sold in US
CF-KJL	715	Stinson 108 Station Wagon	To Brian Gay, Ottawa
CF-PCL	AF-80	Beech D18S	To Sioux Narrows, Winnipeg
CF-BXO		Stranraer	To RAF Museum, Hendon
CF-EIM	F11-2	F11 Husky	To North Coast Air, Prince Rupert
CF-EQP		Bellanca Skyrocket	
CF-. . .		PA-23 Apache	Written off
C-GXVF	c/n 7	DHC-7 Dash 7	To Air Pacific as N27AP
C-GXVG	11	DHC-7 Dash 7	To Air Wisconsin as N791S
CF-CZQ	45078	DC-6A	Leased from Cunard Eagle
CF-CZZ	45498	DC-6A	Leased from Canadian Pacific. To NWT Air
CF-PCI	43555	DC-6B	ex-KLM
CF-FUN (1)	19242	B727-11C	To Cruzeiro as PP-CJI 05.73
CF-FAN	19789	B707-311C	To Kuwait Air as 9K-ACX
CF-ZYP	20043	B707-396C	ex-N1786B. To Montana as OE-IDA
C-FDJC (2)	20208	B747-1D1	Current, ex-Braniff N602BN
C-FFUN (2)	20305	B747-124	Current, ex-Continental N26864
C-GXRA	21516	B747-211B	Current
C-GXRD	21517	B747-211B	Current
C-GXRB	46976	DC-10 Srs 30	Current ex-N8712Q for test only
C-GXRC	46978	DC-10 Srs 30	Current
C-GVYX	292	DHC-4A Caribou	ex-8R-GDR, delivered to Toronto on 08.11.80 for use on northern operations

Below: DC-10 srs 30, C-GXRC *W.R. 'Wop' May* **after its delivery on 8 November 1978.**

Bottom: **Boeing 747-211B, C-GXRD, taxying in to the terminal area after landing at Toronto with an August 1980 arrival.**
Caz Caswell/Flightlines International

By Wardair to Canada

PAUL BEAVER

IF THERE is anything for which the last decade in air transport will be remembered, apart from Concorde, it will be the cheap trans-Atlantic passenger fares.

It is not only the traveller on the high density London-New York sector who has benefited, because remarkably low fares are now available to other Continental United States cities and to Canada. Wardair Canada, formed 27 years ago, now flies from three British airports to six Canadian destinations, including Edmonton in the prairie province of Alberta.

The flight deck of the Boeing 747-200 appears little different from its popular predecessor, the 707. Flying high above the wastes of Arctic Canada, while the other passengers enjoy a traditional steak meal, one is impressed by the cool, efficient and seemingly effortless way in which the three flight deck crew members go about the business of taking C-GXRA *Herbert Hollick-Kenyon* on Track Bravo, and later Lateral Two from London-Gatwick to Edmonton International, by way of Stornoway, Iceland, Greenland and the 'Pine Tree' Line.

'It is not a bus ride', remarks Don Saunders, a young Wardair captain with 17 years' flying for the Company. The three up front, the captain, first officer and flight engineer have to continuously monitor the flight path of Wardair 200; checking the track on one of the three inertial navigation systems ('good to one foot, you know'), calling up the various reporting stations and perhaps more importantly in these days of fuel economy, checking that the speed/height/power mix is perfect.

The Boeing 747, like all Wardair aircraft named after a pioneer of Canadian bush aviation, is 'as responsive as a 727' (remember Gatwick visitor CF-FUN?) with hydraulically assisted flight controls making it a 'sheer delight to fly'. On the ground, however, life is a little more difficult because of the relative position of the flight deck to the rest of the airliner. Taxy speeds need to be controlled carefully, especially on slippery runways and this does make the 'bird' difficult to manoeuvre for the inexperienced flyer. The cockpit level is the highest in any civilian aircraft and before turning, the digital groundspeed read-out must be below 15mph if an embarrassing accident is to be avoided.

We had left the Scottish air traffic control zone at FL390 (39,000ft) and as the fuel was burnt off from the inboard tanks, the aircraft became lighter; we descended to FL370 over Iceland and again down to FL350 over the Polar region. The procedure of burning off fuel by compartment leaves fuel in the outboard tanks as long as possible to assist structural integrity. Not that anyone is unduly worried about that — as first officer and former RCAF pilot Jake Vobe said, 'Boeing builds good, strong aircraft'.

An interesting facet of the Wardair personnel structure is that flight engineers, like Bryan Kozak are very much part of the flight deck crew. Bryan was originally a ground engineer at the Wardair base of Edmonton, and now, like all of the airline's flight engineers he is qualified to sign out the aircraft as fit to fly in the event of any snags down the line. In fact, spares for most eventualities are carried on board.

The same high regard for the airline is felt by the cabin attendants, 'not stewards and stewardesses please'. The flight supervisor on this particular flight was Jane Barry, another Edmontonian who had been with the airline for 8½ years. She was proud of the airline's reputation in Canada for a courteous, efficient service. She thought this was especially important for those using the trans-Atlantic (summer) and Caribbean (winter) flights as these passengers were usually just beginning or ending their holidays. Before joining a flight crew, the flight attendants go to the American Airlines college at Dallas, Tx for a tough, thorough training which has a 75% safety content. The average training period includes four weeks in class with two weeks actually flying on a scheduled service under the watchful eye of more experienced attendants like Jane or Brett Christiansen, another Albertan. There are no plastic smiles for Wardair — they take the inflight service very seriously, from the moment the passenger steps aboard, they're on holiday. But in an emergency, the reactions are automatic; for example, each attendant responsible for an emergency exit has already picked out in his/her mind an able-bodied passenger to assist in 'the unlikely event of an evacuation'. This can cause a few conflicts because the seats near exits usually have the most room and are thus better for handicapped passengers; however such passengers,

Above: **The Wardair Boeing 747 in which the author flew to Edmonton, C-GXRA** *Herbert Hollick-Kenyon,* **on the stand alongside the departure lounge at Gatwick.** *Paul Beaver*

welcome as they are, must be clear of an exit during the hectic moments when the escape gear has to be activated. Just remember that the next time a smiling attendant ushers you to a seat by the exit!

After dinner, all served in china crockery (!) with a selection of house wines, (Wardair reportedly has its own vineyards) I was invited back to the flightdeck for the 120 miles or so let-down into Edmonton.

The final phase of the flight had now begun and with only 102 miles to go (or so said the three digital computers) the flight engineer ran through his checks as the 747 descended from FL370 to FL340. The speed, again available on a digital read-out, drops away and the first officer with route chart in hand, confirmed our status with the regional air traffic controller.

The Prairies stretch as far as the eye can see as we break cloud at FL318 (with only 87 miles to go — it is certainly reassuring to know that the ever-checking flight computer system is accurate to a few hundred yards!) The scenery below soon changes as we approach Edmonton, Canada's major northern city, with its oil refineries and downtown skyscrapers.

During the whole of this carefully executed phase, the captain has been unobtrusive, but all-seeing. A brief comment that the home-town looks good gives the impression that the crew will be glad to exchange places with a fresh contingent for the final sector to Vancouver. The whole of the crew aboard WD200 were Edmonton-based and most were born and bred there.

Edmonton International confirms that we are Number 2 on approach and immediately a swift scan of the horizon is made for the airliner in front of us; it is quickly spotted — an Air Canada DC-9. The tower gives us landing instructions, the wind is a pleasant 5kts at 120° and the last minutes of Flight 200 are filled with checks — instruments, seats and the passenger in the jump-seat.

Suddenly it is all over, we are on the ground after 8hr 29min. We slowly (well, it appears almost painfully slowly) taxy in to the terminal, avoiding a Cherokee which has become lost on the taxi-way.

Wardair take their in-flight service very seriously, every moment the passenger is aboard, but as I was reminded several times during the flight — you're on holiday from the moment you step aboard. I still can't get over being asked how I liked my steak!

Acknowledgement

The author wishes to record his sincere thanks to Wardair and to Captain Don Sauders and his crew for the way in which they assisted with the preparation of this article.

Below: **Leisure Sport's Fokker Dr1 triplane replica, registered G-BEFR, was built in 1977 and has been since then a regular representative of the WW1 period at airshows in the UK.**
Peter R. March

WINGS OF HISTORY

PETER R. MARCH

AT AIR SHOWS up and down the United Kingdom a rich cavalcade of aviation history is portrayed by enthusiastic private pilots week after week during the summer months. Nowhere else in the world can aircraft ranging through the whole of the 75 years of powered flight in Europe be seen in the air. The great majority of these unique original and replica machines are owned and operated by individuals or civilian organisations like the Shuttleworth Trust, Personal Plane Services and Leisure Sport.

Without the many hours spent preparing these aircraft and the devotion of most weekends by the pilots concerned, the air displays that attract such huge crowds would be very much the poorer. The participation by the Royal Navy, the Army and the Royal Air Force is professional and spectacular, but makes up quite a small part of the air fetes, galas, flying days, air pageants and air fairs at places from Bodmin to Prestwick and Little Snoring to Swansea.

The oldest flying participants come from the Shuttleworth Trust at Old Warden, with the 1909 original Bleriot XI and 1910 Bristol Boxkite replica. World War 1 is well represented by adversaries like the Morane Type N and Fokker E3 from Personal Plane Services and Sopwith Camel and Fokker Drl Triplane from Leisure Sport. The inter-war years are typified by the magnificent Fairey Flycatcher replica from John Fairey, 1927 Supermarine S5 replica which is usually flown by Keith Sissons, the rare Blackburn B2 and from the age of the great air races, the Mew Gull and Hawk Speed Six.

The WW2 years can boast many of the significant types still airworthy. Spitfires, Hurricanes, Mosquito, Mitchell, Flying Fortress and support aircraft like Dominies, Proctor and Lysander are regularly put

Above: **The Bristol Boxkite replica, BAPC-2, which starred as 'The Phoenix Flyer' in the film** *Those Magnificent Men in their Flying Machines,* **is flown from Old Warden airfield by the Shuttleworth Trust.**
All photos by Peter R. March, unless otherwise credited

through their paces in the hands of Tony Bianchi, Jeff Hawke and Keith Sissons. *Luftwaffe* types are not quite so numerous but the incredible STOL Fiesler Storch and Messerschmitt Bf108 Taifun are represented by French-built variants.

Moving on to the postwar era, enthusiasts like Jim Buckingham from the Bristol Plane Preservation Group keep the Miles Messenger and Gemini on the airshow circuit, alongside a great range of types like the Anson, Pembroke, Varsity, YAK-18 and Sea Fury from all over the country in the capable hands of their owner-pilots. Rotorcraft are not left out either. Major Mike Somerton-Rayner flies his Saro Skeeter in a ground hopping routine reminiscent of the days it was in use with the Army Air Corps as a spotter helicopter. An ever popular performer is Ken Wallis in his autogyro 'Little Nellie', which re-enacts its starring role as a mount for 007 James Bond, while British Airways TriStar captain John Kitchen shows what the Campbell Cricket can do.

Aerobatic displays not only show the skills of the various pilots like Richard Goode, Bob Mitchell and Phillip Meeson but also introduce some fascinating aircraft. Although the Pitts S1 and S2 are most frequently seen the Ryan PT-26, Stephens Akro, Zlin

65

526 and Cranfield A-1 also appear. While aerobatic teams come and go the Tiger Club has for many years provided its own distinctive input. Mirror aerobatics by Stampes and wing-tied formations of Turbulents are regular contributions to many shows.

It might be easy to dismiss the solo displays by a scarlet Hunter as being a service contribution — but it is not. Hunter Mk 51, G-HUNT, is owned by businessman Spencer Flack and is flown from Cranfield to airshows in the UK and Europe. With the appearance of British Aerospace's demonstrator Harrier, G-VTOL, and Hawk G-HAWK, from time to time, we have come right up to date with the jet aircraft of the eighties. From a rich aviation heritage there is a healthy legacy which brings the wings of history right into your local airshow in 1982.

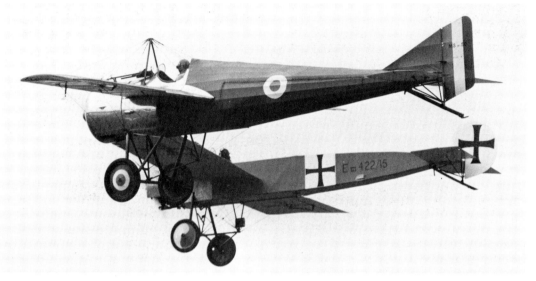

Above: **Two replicas that feature in airshow representations of WW1 aerial combat are the Morane Type N (nearer the camera) built in 1969 by Personal Plane Services at Booker and the 1965-built (by the same company) Fokker E3.**

Below: **The LVG CVI, one of the magnificent aircraft to be seen flying at the Shuttleworth events at Old Warden, near Biggleswade, Beds.**

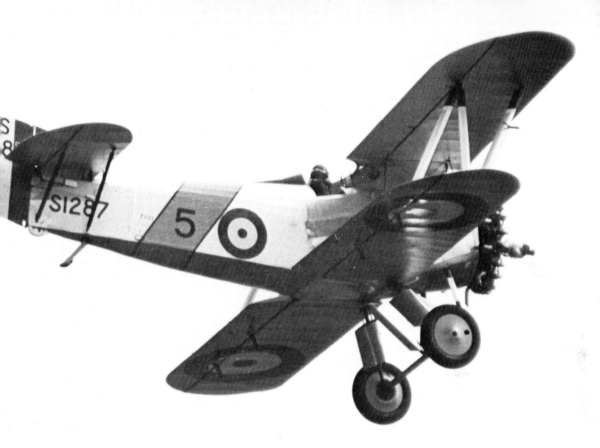

Above: **The inter-war period of naval aviation is recaptured by the Fairey Flycatcher, here flown by John Fairey at Middle Wallop in July 1979.**

Centre left: **Not a duel for the 1950 King's Cup Air Race but a nostalgic pylon turn by Hawk Speed 6, G-ADGP, and Mew Gull, G-AEXF, at the Shuttleworth Air Pageant in September 1980.**

Bottom left: **The Blackburn B2 is preserved at Brough, North Humberside by British Aerospace and flies regularly at airshows in the Midlands and North of England.**

Above: **Tony Bianchi flying Hon Patrick Lindsay's Spitfire IA, AR213 (G-AIST), in fine style from its base at Booker.**

Top left: **Also owned by Hon Patrick Lindsay and kept at Booker is the Morane 500, G-AZMH, a noted STOL performer on the airshow circuit.**
Andrew March

Top right: **One of the best known and favourite attractions at UK air events, the B-17G Flying Fortress** *Sally B,* **which has been based at Duxford since its arrival from France in March 1975.**

Above: **The Miles Gemini 1A, G-AKKB, here flown by Jim Buckingham, was restored to flying condition by the Bristol Plane Preservation Unit between 1977-79.**
Andrew March

Left: **The Tiger Club from Redhill are long-established exponents of the aerobatic art at European airshows; this view shows an impressive 'mirror' display by two Tiger Club Stampe biplanes at the Biggin Hill International Air Fair.**

Above right: **The Saro Skeeter AOP12 light observation helicopter, XM553, puts on a lively display in the hands of Mike Somerton Rayner.**

Right: **John Kitchen, a British Airways TriStar captain, flies his Super Cricket gyrocopter as part of the British Airways display team.**

Above: **A new 'solo' Pitts Special at airshows in 1980 was G-SOLO flown by David Perrin, seen at Badminton, Glos in July of that year.**

Centre right: **The Stephens Akro, G-RIDE, flown by Bob Mitchell.**

Below right: **Spencer Flack's Hunter F51, G-HUNT, first appeared on the airshow scene in mid-1980 and has since been a colourful participant (the aircraft is painted red overall) at numerous shows.** *Andrew March*

THE Royal Air Force Museum exists on voluntary funds, and one of the chief sources of revenue is the sale of souvenir flown postal covers which are produced in series form, based on the commemoration of particular events connected with aviation.

The information and illustrations presented by these colourful covers provide an interesting and informative background into the history of aviation. The aspiring collector can get a glimpse into the past glories of the Royal Air Force and also of the legendary pioneer civilian aviators.

After the Post Office produced a stamp in 1968 to celebrate the 50th Anniversary of the Royal Air Force, various stations produced souvenir envelopes to mark the occasion. After that year all the Royal Air Force philatelic activity was co-ordinated by the Royal Air Force Museum's public relations officer, with the aim of raising funds for the Museum.

There are three types of cover for each issue: the Ordinary Cover, the Pilot Signed Cover and the Special. Several of the covers issued in the various series have become rare collector's items and a great many covers have appreciated significantly in value.

The RAF Museum's flown covers

The first series of covers depicts famous aircraft flown by the RNAS, the Royal Flying Corps and the Royal Air Force from various RAF stations, the aircraft ranging from the BE2 of 1912 to the Gloster Meteor of 1945.

The second series commemorates the history of 40 squadrons of the RAF. The co-ordinated series of covers which stations of the Royal Air Force have produced themselves cover events such as station closures and first and last flights of service aircraft.

The air display series covers aerobatic teams, helicopter display teams and parachute teams, both military and civil, either in the United Kingdom or Europe.

The Royal Air Force Escaping Society covers are produced by the Museum and they depict escapes which have taken place from the countries concerned. So far there have been 20 covers in this series. The latest series of covers being issued are those dealing with historic aviators. The first cover in the series depicts Mitchell, the designer of the Spitfire. The Battle of Britain aces have been honoured, as have the two famous women pilots, Amy Johnson and Jean Batten. This series also includes world-famous airmen like Lindbergh from the USA, Billy Bishop from Canada and Kingsford Smith from Australia.

Altogether over 200 covers have now been produced, and a list giving information of covers still obtainable, together with information of new covers produced, is available*. The income from the sale of new covers has been of great help in meeting the cost of the Battle of Britain Museum which was constructed on a site adjacent to the existing Museum, and opened by HM Queen Elizabeth, the Queen Mother, in November, 1978.

*Information regarding covers and badges can be obtained from Flt Lt F. W. Waters, RAFVR(T), Royal Air Force Museum, Hendon. Telephone Number: 01-205 2266, Ext 34.

No XV SQUADRON
ROYAL AIR FORCE

60th Anniversary of the Formation of the Squadron 1st March 1975

BE2c 1915

SHORT STIRLING Mk1
MACROBERT'S REPLY. N6086
No15 SQN.RAF OCT.1941-WYTON
4-1,650 H.P.BRISTOL HERCULES 16
MAX SPEED
270 M.PH.AT 14,500 FT.

LS○F

H.S.BUCCANEER S2B 1975

AUGUST MACKE 1887-1914
DEUTSCHE BUNDESPOST
30

Flown on route Laarbruch, Wyton, Brest, Wyton, Laarbruch on February 17th, 1975. On December 18th, 1941, "MacRobert's Reply" was one of nine XV Squadron Stirlings that flew from Wyton to Brest harbour to bomb the SCHARNHORST, PRINZ EUGEN and GNEISENAU.

Flown in Buccaneer S2B XX 888, 'C'.
Pilot: Flt Lt A M Taylor; Navigator: Flt Lt G A Coop
Flight Time: 2 hrs 51 mins.

Officer Commanding
4179 Weeze
Flugplatz Laarbruch

HER MAJESTY
THE QUEEN'S
SILVER JUBILEE REVIEW
OF THE
ROYAL AIR FORCE

Flown in a Fly Past at Royal Air Force, Finningley to mark Her Majesty the Queen's Silver Jubilee Review of the Royal Air Force.

Aircraft:	Dominie T1 XS 739
Captain:	Sqn. Ldr. R. D. Downs RAF
Co-Pilot:	Flt. Lt. M. A. Pickthall RAF
Navigators:	Flt. Lt. A. S. Nussey RAF
	Flt. Lt. R. Patterson RAF
Flight Time:	1 hour 30 minutes

Officer Commanding
Royal Air Force
Finningley

ROYAL AIR FORCES
ESCAPING SOCIETY
DUKE OF YORK'S HQ LONDON S.W.3

RAFES SC 21

香
港
逃
亡

Flown in Wessex HC 5, XR 500 of No 28 Sqn from Royal Air Force Kai Tak, to a position over the Government Stadium, Happy Valley, Hong Kong, from where it was dropped in a free fall parachute descent by the Red Devils as part of the Pageant for the Hong Kong Commemoration of Her Queen's Silver Jubilee. The drop was made at night (1345 hrs) into the Stadium from a height of 4500 ft. Parachuting time 2 mins 15 secs of which 10 secs was in free fall.

RED DEVILS —

CPL. R. KALINSKI	Parachute Regt. (Jump Master)
CPT. M. MUNN	Parachute Regt.
CPT. N. O'BRIEN	Army Air Corps.
FLT. SGT. K. MAPPLEBECK	Royal Air Force
CPL. A. SINCLAIR	Parachute Regt.
L. CPL. J. STREET	Parachute Regt.
PTE. K. HOLMES	Parachute Regt.
PTE. C. RILEY	Parachute Regt.

F/O B. Fawcett
R.H.K.A.A.F.
R.A.F. Kai Tak
KOWLOON

Group Captain
Sir DOUGLAS BADER
CBE, DSO, DFC

RAFM HA20

THE
H.G. HAWKER
ENGINEERING Cº
LIMITED
KINGSTON on THAMES

40TH
ANNIVERSARY
FIRST FLIGHT
OF PRODUCTION
HURRICANE

12 OCTOBER 77

BRITISH FORCES 1593 POSTAL SERVICE

8P

No 242 SQN LED BY
S/LDR DOUGLAS BADER
CLIMBS INTO ACTION
SEPTEMBER 1940

FLOWN IN HAWKER SIDDELEY 125 MK 1, XW 789
ON THE OCCASION OF THE 40th ANNIVERSARY OF
THE FIRST FLIGHT OF THE PRODUCTION HAWKER
HURRICANE L 1547 FROM BROOKLANDS, 12th
OCTOBER 1937. FROM ROYAL AIR FORCE NORTHOLT
- FRANKFURT - BERLIN (GATOW) - COPENHAGEN
- STUTTGART - GRENOBLE - PARIS (ORLY) -
CLERMONT FERRAND - AMSTERDAM - AALBORG -
RAF NORTHOLT.

CAPTAINS: SQN. LDR. H. O. HOOD, RAF.
            FLT. LT. G. W. RIPPIN, RAF.

TOTAL FLYING TIME: 12 HRS. 50 MINS.

Officer Commanding
Royal Air Force
Northolt
Middlesex

THE BARNSTORMERS

THE
BARNSTORMERS
FLYING CIRCUS

FLYING
CIRCUS

THE BARNSTORMERS

G-ANOH

RAFA
50TH
ANNIVERSARY
Air Show
SYWELL

27 MAY 78

BRITISH FORCES 1616 POSTAL SERVICE

7P

FLOWN BY THE BARNSTORMERS DURING THE SYWELL
50th ANNIVERSARY AIR SHOW IN DH TIGER MOTH G-AVPJ.

"Girl on Wing"	Pilot: Mr. B. Tempest	Flt. Time: 11 mins.
"Glider Tow-off"	Pilot: Mr. B. Tempest	Flt. Time: 9 mins.
"Crackshot"	Pilot: Mr. B. Tempest	Flt. Time: 12 mins.
"Limbo"	Pilot: Mr. A. Harold	Flt. Time: 11 mins.
"Streamer Cutting"	Pilot: Mr. B. Tempest	Flt. Time: 10 mins.
"Battle Piece"	Pilot: Mr. B. Tempest	Flt. Time: 12 mins.

SYWELL
50th ANNIVERSARY AIR SHOW
28/29 MAY 1978

RAF Museum
Aerodrome Road
Hendon NW9 5LL

Navy Helos on the Rock

TONY FAIRBAIRN

Above: **Wessex HAS3, XP150, from the HMS**
***Antrim* Flight of No 737 Naval Air Squadron at RAF**
Gibraltar on 29 May 1980.
All photos in this article by the author

YOU DO NOT have to be in Gibraltar very long to realise what an important place it is in Naval terms. Its key position at the entrance to the Mediterranean, a bustling dockyard with repair and refit facilities, and weather that is ideal for exercises and training all combine to produce a steady flow of Naval vessels engaged in a wide variety of tasks. The helicopters carried by many of these vessels, such as frigates, destroyers and Royal Fleet Auxiliaries (RFAs), are frequent visitors to the RAF airfield on 'The Rock', making brief calls for mail and passengers but also disembarking for longer periods to carry out maintenance and flying training which cannot be done at sea.

The majority of the visiting helicopters are Royal Navy aircraft comprising Wasps, Lynx, Sea Kings and Wessex, taking advantage of the engineering and other support facilities available at the RAF base. On rare occasions there are more Navy helicopters than RAF aircraft on the station and in such cases the RN pilots have not been slow in referring to 'RNAS Gibraltar'! But helicopters from other navies also make appearances, giving an international flavour to this junction of the world's waterways.

The Wasp and its replacement, the Lynx, outnumber the other types and carry out fairly similar work to each other while disembarked from their parent warships. The aircrews must complete a prescribed number of flying hours per month including both day and night continuation training. This is broken down into torpedo dropping, missile firing, carrying underslung loads, and winching. Ships' divers are often winched out of the water after making an underwater inspection of the vessel in harbour. In addition to these purely Navy tasks the more powerful and more versatile Lynx occasionally performs a useful additional function on behalf of the Army, that of providing helicopter troop drills for the resident infantry battalion in Gibraltar. This involves emplaning troops at RAF Gibraltar and flying them to an area on the Rock for a tactical deployment. Emergency helicopter drills can also be practised. The useful range of the Lynx was highlighted recently when a German TV camera crew making a documentary on Gibraltar was flown 50 miles out to sea to film a frigate making live firings.

Left: **Helicopters from allied navies are also frequent visitors to the Rock — seen here is an Italian Navy Agusta-Bell AB 212ASW, MM80957, which had come ashore from the frigate** *Carabiniere.*

Below: **Westland Wasp HAS1, XT784 from HMS** *Scylla* **— beyond are another Wasp, from HMS** *Active* **and a Wessex from the County class destroyer HMS** *Kent.*

Bottom: **Royal Navy Sea King HAS2, XV698, of B Flight No 824 Naval Air Squadron assigned to the Royal Fleet Auxiliary** *Fort Austin.*

Still looking immaculate after a career spanning 19 years, the Wessex, operating in both the transport and the anti-submarine roles, made frequent appearances during the spring of 1980. Individual Wessex HU5s are embarked on RFAs, such as *Tidespring*, to provide vertical logistic support for the Fleet. In addition, two HU5s of No 845 Sqn operating in the commando role from the assault ship HMS *Intrepid* took part in the RAF Gibraltar Open Day on 10 May 1980 and one of these, XT481/E gave a sparkling demonstration of flying and troop emplanement. The anti-submarine version on the other hand, the HAS3, has been something of a rarity but was represented in late-May by a solitary aircraft, XP150/406 from HMS *Antrim*.

As the exercise activity in the waters around Gibraltar increases so the helicopter flying gets busier. It was two springtime exercises in 1980 that brought 'the heavy mob' to the Rock in the shape of Sea Kings of No 824 Sqn. This unit, which was earlier embarked on HMS *Ark Royal*, was split into flights of two aircraft each when the carrier was retired. The flights were then allocated to RFAs, such as the *Olmeda*, *Fort Austin* and *Fort Grange*, where and when required. The first major exercise of 1980 took place in March, during which the Sea Kings deployed approximately 70 miles to the east of Gibraltar to carry out sonar work with a task group. One aircraft, XV698/581, flew an impressive average of 16hr/day.

The other exercise, a NATO one a few weeks later, produced a flurry of Canadian Sikorsky CH-124s (Sea Kings) ferrying stores, mail and passengers to and from Gibraltar. These particular aircraft were from the Canadian destroyer *Athabaskan* and the frigate *Annapolis*.

Left: **Close-up view of the nose markings on another Sea King assigned to the RFA *Fort Austin* — this one, XZ577, having been dubbed *The Bitch*.**

Below: **Replacing the Wasp helicopters in the RN's small ships flights, the Westland Lynx HAS2 — this one, XZ238, displaying the SS code of the frigate HMS *Sirius*.**

Bottom: **Canadian Forces Sikorksy CH-124 (a version of the SH-3A Sea King) of No 443 Squadron from HMCS *Annapolis* visiting Gibraltar in April 1980.**

North American Amphibians

AIRCRAFT THAT are capable of taking off and alighting on water – flying boats, seaplanes, floatplanes, etc – have always enjoyed a particular appeal in the aviation world. The challenge of producing machines with this ability is obvious, and it has occupied many famous designers and companies, among the latter being the US manufacturer Grumman whose products are largely featured on these pages. The appeal of these aircraft rests,

perhaps, in the sense of freedom they embody in not being tied to operating from discrete runway surfaces; or possibly it is the enhanced sense of contact with the elements enjoyed by the passengers, the visual impact of the aircraft's passage across the water on take-off and landing. Operationally the most flexible of these machines is the amphibian, equally at home on land or water. This selection of photographs shows some of the examples to be seen in North America.

Top: **West Coast Air Services Grumman G-73 Mallard at Vancouver, BC.**

Above: **Further down the apron at Vancouver International Airport was this Grumman G-21 Goose, C-FHUZ.**

Photographs by RONALD HERON

Below: **Based at Orange County Airport, Santa Ana, Ca, is Trans Catalina Airlines with three Mallards (and a Piper Navajo Chieftain); this is N36DF named** *Spirit of Avalon.*

Below: Floatplanes in the guise of amphibians — two DHC6 Twin Otters of the Province of Ontario's Ministry of Natural Resources rest on their beaching wheels; the nearer aircraft is C-FOPJ.

Bottom: This time a real example of the amphibian at work as a Grumman G-21A Goose, N22932, of Catalina Airlines Inc comes ashore at San Pedro, Ca in July 1979.

F·16 Fighting Falcon

CLEARLY SET to become the Western World's most numerically important fighter purchase in the 1980s, the General Dynamics F-16 acquired its long awaited identity in 1980 with the announcement that the manufacturers and customers had finally settled on the name 'Fighting Falcon' for the compact, multi-role derivative of the USAF lightweight fighter (LWF) programme. First flown in YF-16 prototype form in February 1974, and winner of the competitive LWF fly-off with the Northrop YF-17, it was in early-1975 that the USAF decided to proceed with a combat version of the GD design as the Air Combat Fighter (ACF) to replace the F-4 Phantom in air-to-ground roles and supplement the F-15 Eagle in air-to-air missions. Later that year the F-16 became an international programme with the decision by four European countries (Belgium, the Netherlands, Norway and Denmark) to buy 348 of the aircraft and join General Dynamics in a co-production venture, which would also see the procurement of 650 F-16s by the US. In fact, the planned purchase for the USAF has risen to 1,388 and anticipated 'second buys' on the part of the European Participating Governments (EPG) could increase their offtake to over 600 aircraft. In 'third country' markets – those outside the five-nation production partnership – sales have been made to Israel (75) and Egypt (40); and South Korea is planning an initial buy of 36. Additionally the Fighting Falcon is short-listed for procurement decisions in other countries such as Australia, Spain and Austria.

Top: **Plan view of the F-16 illustrated by an early-production single seater at Edwards AFB, Ca in November 1977.**

Above: **F-16As and Bs of the Multi-national Operational Test and Evaluation (MOT&E) detachment at Hill AFB, Ut, home of the USAF's first front-line unit to receive the type, the 388th TFW.** *F. B. Mormillo*

Below: **An F-16A of the Royal Netherlands Air Force, J-215, displays its underside grey paint scheme during a climbing turn.** *RNethAF*

Above left: **An F-16A from Detachment 16 of the Tactical Fighter Weapons Center lands at Nellis AFB, Nv. The aircraft carries wingtip-mounted Sidewinder AAMs, underwing practice bomb containers, a centreline ECM pod and intake-attached Pave Penny laser tracker pod.**

Left: **F-16As from Det16 break for a landing at Nellis AFB.** *Both: F. B. Mormillo*

Below: **A view of the Belgian F-16 assembly line at SABCA's Gosselies works showing the third F-16A and second F-16B for the Belgian Air Force. The SABCA assembly line and its Dutch counterpart at Fokker's Schiphol plant will each complete 174 aircraft of the initially planned EPG F-16 requirement, those produced in Belgium going to the Belgian Air Force (116) and the Royal Danish Air Force (58).** *SA Belge de Constructions Aeronautiques (SABCA)*

Left: **The first two-seat F-16B for the Belgian Air Force outside the SABCA plant. The Service's initial examples of the Fighting Falcon were handed over to No 349 Squadron of the 1st Fighter Wing at Beauvechain AB in May 1979.**
SABCA

Centre left: **F-16s on the Fokker assembly line at Schiphol, which is initially scheduled to deliver 102 aircraft to the RNethAF and 72 to the Royal Norwegian Air Force.**
Fokker

Bottom left: **The first production F-16B two seater, s/n 75-0751, landing at Edwards AFB, Ca.**
F. B. Mormillo

Right: **F-16A carrying the all-weather combat information pod (AWCIP) and Sidewinder missiles.**
F. B. Mormillo

Below: **The first two-seater delivered to the RNethAF was J-259 which went to the conversion flight at Leeuwarden AB tasked with the introduction of the type to Nos 322 and 323 Squadrons.**
RNethAF

Above right: **Air-to-ground missile armament on an F-16A with six AGM-65 Maverick rounds on its wing pylons.**

Centre right: **The fourth production F-16A, s/n 75-0748 lands at Edwards AFB, Ca.**

Below: **An F-16B of the 16th TFTS/388th TFW being pre-flighted at Hill AFB, Ut.** *F. B. Mormillo*

Above: **An F-16B at Nellis AFB in February 1980 and carrying Sidewinder missiles, 2,000lb bombs and a centreline ECM pod.** *F. B. Mormillo*

Right: **RNethAF F-16A Fighting Falcon, J-212. After conversion of Nos 322 and 323 Squadrons in 1980-81, the Dutch Air Force will introduce the type to the three Volkel AB squadrons, Nos 311, 312 and 306. The latter will remain a tactical reconnaissance unit, as it has been with the RF-104G Starfighter, but all the other four units will fulfil a common role — air superiority and tactical air support.** *Fokker*

Right: An F-16B, J-261, of the RNethAF in its shelter at Leeuwarden AB.

Below: The first trials of the Orpheus reconnaissance pod, destined for continued RNethAF use on No 306 Squadron F-16s, were made with J-216, also wearing the squadron's badge to mark the occasion. *RNethAF*

Above: An F-16A for the Royal Norwegian Air Force seen at Schiphol prior to delivery. The aircraft are fitted with brake parachutes to facilitate winter operations in Norway, the 'chute being housed in the rearwards extension at the base of the fin.

Centre left: This landing shot of a RNorAF F-16B shows the brake parachute housing in profile view. *Both: Fokker*

Bottom left: A 1980 F-16 visitor to the UK was the B model which took part in the Farnborough Show equipped with wingtip smoke generators.
Peter Gilchrist

'Shifting a Lanc'

W. OLDENAMPSEN

THE AIR FORCE Association in Australia is a national organisation, which exists mainly to support and look after the interests of retired RAAF personnel. The Western Australia Branch of the AFA, for example, maintains a large estate near the city of Perth and on this site a number of two-storey flats have been built as accommodation for Air Force veterans. The estate also provides amentity facilities for outdoor sports as well as living quarters.

About eight years ago the then-secretary of the AFA, Mr Frank Purser, started a collection of historical aviation items and in the process he went on to found an Aviation Historical Group as part of the AFA. From these tentative beginnings there has been drawn together a band of devoted aviation preservation enthusiasts, with an acknowledged position in historical aviation matters in Australia. The efforts of the Group have been realised most notably in the establishment of an Aviation Museum. Pride of place in the Museum's collection goes to an Avro Lancaster, NX622 — this is the story of its relocation to the Museum and of the development of the Museum itself.

There are two 'Lancs' in Australia; one is 'G for George' housed in Canberra Museum and the other one is NX622 in Western Australia. 'Our' aircraft came off the production line in May 1945 and is one of the 180 Mk VII Lancasters built under contract by Austin Motors. It was then delivered to No 38 Maintenance Unit of the RAF and in the following month transferred to No 32 MU. In December 1945 the aircraft was returned to the builders for modification and went back to No 38 MU after the work was completed. In 1951 the aircraft was sent to A. V. Roe and Co for conversion to the maritime reconnaissance role prior to transfer to the French Navy under the 'Western Union' arrangements. It was in June 1952 that the aircraft was officially taken over by the *Aeronautique Navale* and re-serialled WU 16. After a few years of service with various squadrons and completion of 1,200hr flying time, the aircraft was given a major overhaul by UAT at Le Bourget. Subsequently issued to *Escadrille 9 S*, the Lancaster was flown out to its new Base at Tontouta, New Caledonia, in the Pacific. The aircraft operated with this squadron from 1957 until 1962, after which she was withdrawn from service.

The West Australian Air Force Association made an approach to the French Authorities in an effort to obtain the Lancaster and after many months of negotiations, during which a number of seemingly insurmountable problems were overcome, the matter was finally settled. On 29 November 1962, the Lancaster, under the command of Captain Henri Martini, left Noumea for Australia. After overnight stops at Sydney and Adelaide, the aircraft finally

appeared over the city of Perth on Saturday 1 December 1962 at 13.00hrs. She made a circuit over the Perth Metropolitan area and Perry Lakes Stadium (it was the closing day of the VII Commonwealth Games) and then landed at Perth Airport. The aircraft was painted white overall and carried French Navy roundels.

On account of the Lanc's size, the then Department of Civil Aviation made some land available to the AFA behind the main terminal building at the airport, and it was to this site that the aircraft was transferred in due course. The AFA erected a wire fence around the aircraft for its protection and with time the Lanc became a notable landmark.

The task of maintaining the Lancaster for static display was initially handled by the AFA itself but later delegated to the Historical Group, and the aircraft was repainted in the camouflage colours of the RAAF. Teams of our members volunteered their time on Sunday afternoons to open the compound to the public. A small charge was made and the revenues received were used in turn for the aircraft's upkeep as well as for other restoration projects the Group had on hand.

In 1978, the AFA was informed by the Department of Transport (formerly the Dept of Civil Aviation) that the aircraft was to be removed because the site it occupied was required for the Perth Airport expansion programme. Bearing in mind that the aircraft had been standing out in the open for the best part of 15 years, one can well imagine the delicacy as well as the enormity of the project that then had to be contemplated. The AFA asked the Historical Group to take over the task. In consultation with the Group it had been decided to bring the aircraft to the AFA Estate.

A small 'task force' was formed from the Group members and headed by Mr Bill Gimson, a retired aircraft engineer formerly employed by Ansett Airlines in Perth. The task confronting the team was the biggest undertaken so far; although we had a fair idea how to go about the job, numerous problems cropped up and had to be solved. The Group's first objective was to obtain a Lancaster Manual. As none was available in our extensive library, a photo-copy of the Manual was ordered from England. The next step was to plan a work procedure. It was decided to remove all the props, the two outer Merlin engines, the two outer wing-sections and both elevators. Our task force was then divided into small two or three-man teams, each with an allotted job.

One of the first problems related to the special tools required. It is all very well to say 'remove the props' but quite another matter when it comes to actually doing it. There was no spanner large enough to loosen

Right: **The Lancaster's port outer ready for removal – facing the camera is engineer Bill Gimson.**

Below right: **Removal of the aircraft's starboard wing.**

the prop nuts. It was in this sphere that our Engineer's former contacts became extremely useful. Our team received tremendous co-operation from the workshops of Ansett Airlines, Trans Australia Airlines and Qantas Airways. They lent us the equipment we needed such as proper maintenance ladders and platforms, and their workshops made the various special tools we required — prop tube spanners, lifting lugs, bolt withdrawal tools, spar support brackets, etc.

One very tiresome job which had tempers flaring was that of removing the hundreds of screws which held the various cover plates. Most of the screwheads were filled with paint. Those underneath the aircraft (and out of the rain) were not so bad but the screws holding on the coverplate between the centre section and the outer wing section were a nightmare. In the end we purchased a couple of impact screwdrivers in order to remove them but some two dozen still had to be drilled out.

Every Saturday for six months the team worked on the aircraft. We gained a fair amount of publicity from the media, which at various times appeared with TV cameras to record the removal of one component or another. These films were used in the News broadcasts and in the end, the TV stations gave us most of their film for our archives so that we have a fairly comprehensive record of this project. The author also made a 20min movie of the operation.

From the West Australian Railways we borrowed a number of wooden railway sleepers in order to support the aircraft when required. Another company lent us some scaffolding which we erected under each wing section, and old tyres were gainfully employed as packing. This was a safety measure because with the two outer engines removed, we did not know what might happen when one of the outer wing sections was detached. Perth Airport can be a windy place at times and for all we knew, there might have been too much weight on the one side with possible disastrous results. The Manual told us a lot but did not mention anything on this particular matter!

It may be of interest to note that even after 15 years, the four Merlins had plenty of compression! Some years ago, consideration was given to the feasibility of getting the engines running again. However, this plan did not materialise as the Department of Civil Aviation refused to give permission. Rumour had it that the refusal was based on the possibility of the airframe breaking up! After severing all the connections and draining the oil from the engines, the Nos 1 and 4 units were removed with the use of a mobile crane and moved to the store in our new workshop on the Estate.

Both elevators were slowly removed after we had built a support structure with the railway sleepers. At the same time a structure was built to support the rear of the fuselage. Although the mainwheels had been braced by specially made steel stands, this was not the case with the tailwheel. The tyre had gone flat and the weight of the aircraft caused the tailwheel to bury itself into the soft ground. Bell Brothers Michelin Tyre Co repaired the tyre and also removed the 'flat' spot. The tailwheel oleo is clamped between the two

95

elevators which are bolted together inside the aircraft. A special steel frame was designed and made by our member John Harris to secure the oleo as the author's plan was to tow the plane from that point.

The outer wing sections are joined to the centre section by four large bolts and nuts. The grease used when the aircraft was assembled was clearly visible but, as one can well imagine, it had hardened over the period of 15 years. In our workshop we made special driving punches though it still required the use of a heavy hammer to shift these bolts. All of them were thoroughly cleaned up and reconditioned in the workshops of Ansett Airlines.

A special main spar support bracket was made and used in conjunction with a big Boeing 747 hydraulic jack which we 'borrowed' from Qantas Airways. The jack was needed to lift the mainwheels and to remove the special steel stands. The wheel was then dropped and handed over to the tyre company for inspection. As the hydraulic jack was the only one 'in captivity' in Western Australia, our Engineer and the team members duly said their evening prayers hoping that no 747 arrived at Perth Airport with tyre trouble! Our prayers must have been answered for the jack was used for over a week and nobody woke us up during the night requesting its return.

The mainwheels were found to be in reasonable condition. It was thought that the tubes might have perished but the tyre company advised that they were better than the ones they had in stock! The tyres themselves showed some cracks in the treads, probably caused by the varying weather conditions to which they had been exposed. However, the advice given was that they would last the 15 miles or so from the Airport to the AFA Estate. We also made inquiries with the RAAF to see if we could borrow some Lincoln bomber wheels or tyres but we were informed that none were available. The tyre company then disclosed that their parent company, one of the largest earthmoving concerns in Australia, used similar tyres on their water trailers employed in road construction projects. This was good news as at least we would have a spare on hand in case we had a puncture during the journey.

All parts, bolts and nuts, etc, were carefully marked, numbered and packed in plastic bags and taken to our workshop at the AFA Estate. Some years ago, the Group made its own tandem axle trailer which then came in handy to transport the engines and larger items of equipment — there is no doubt that a trailer is essential to the inventory of any team involved in this type of activity.

The Group's chairman, Mr Ken Hobbs, made a preliminary survey of the route with the Police Traffic Department, and the author — having been connected for many years with the transport industry and being assigned responsibility for the move — made his own survey on a Sunday morning at 05.00hrs and took measurements of all the road intersections, the height of the overhead traffic lights etc. A scale plan was made of the aircraft and the truck-and-dolly combination. The tandem axle dolly was needed because with the two Brownings sticking out of the rear turret, it required at least a space of 11-12ft to have free movement behind the prime mover. I also designed and made the work plan for a special turntable to be fitted in the tailwheel fork and making use of the original tailwheel axle. According to the

Below: **Flight engineer Paul seems to be asking 'How do we put it all back together again'; note the scaffolding and the mainwheels still on their steel stands.**

plan, the total length of the combination came to 97ft. The height to the top of the cockpit was 17½ft and the width of the aircraft standing on its mainwheels was 24ft.

Bearing all this information, I went to see Mr Brian Beaton of the Mains Roads Department, one of the authorities which had to sanction the transport. During the conversation with Mr Beaton, it turned out that he had done his war time service on Lancasters! The MRD was not too happy about the Lancaster being moved on its own wheels and was particularly concerned about the tyres. I informed them that the aircraft had been standing on its own wheels for over a fortnight without showing any signs of losing air pressure. They agreed that the planned method of shifting the aircraft was the obvious way to do the job, and once the MRD was convinced that we had catered for all eventualities, they readily gave their consent. Mr Beaton and his staff gave us their full co-operation, and after the shift had been completed, it was most rewarding to hear the MRD expressing the view that the 'Group had done its homework extremely well!'.

Our chairman, Mr K. Hobbs, then took the matter up with the Traffic Authority, which also approved the transport — though not before giving us some anxious moments.

The Directors of the transport company, Bellway Pty Ltd, gave the writer their full support and promised to provide whatever was necessary. Their workshops made up the special turntable and a new tail stand for the aircraft plus various minor pieces of equipment. The main airport at Perth is located close to the city, and the road over which the Lancaster had to travel lay a few hundred yards from the end of the main runway. The Group enjoyed a good liaison with the Department of Transport — the controlling authority at the airport — and providing the circuit was clear for a few hours, permission was given for us to use the main runway as an access route to get the aircraft out to the road. Needless to say, the co-operation of the Department in these arrangements was much appreciated.

During the six months it took to dismantle the Lancaster we had enjoyed very good to reasonable weather. However, on the day of the actual move, Saturday 18 August 1979, the weather was terrible. Black clouds appeared overhead and the heavens opened up as if to express their discontent that the Lancaster was being moved from its favourite spot after 15 years' residence.

By 09.00hrs most of the Group's members were present at the airport. Team members Max Driscoll and John Haris, both men of many talents, had already made preparations for the removal of the mesh fence surrounding the aircraft. With the help of a few more members, it did not take long before that job was completed. At 10.00hrs two semi-trailers and a big slewing crane from Bellway Pty Ltd arrived on the dot. Under the supervision of our engineer, Bill Gimson, each trailer was loaded with a wing section, one rudder, an elevator and two props plus some ancillary gear. During the process we gathered quite a crowd of onlookers and the media were also present and busy filming. The service truck from the tyre company arrived and a few more pounds of air were pumped into the tyres. The big crane then lifted the tail of the aircraft and swung it around so that the

Below: **With the crane suspended sling holding up the rear fuselage, the dolly is positioned beneath.**

special turntable could be fitted. In order to reduce the strain on the tailwheel oleo, two solid steel brackets were bolted onto the mainspar from which chain and binders were hooked up to the oleo.

The Kenworth prime-mover and dolly from Bellway Pty Ltd arrived by midday and the special turntable was hooked up to the turntable of the dolly, which was secured in a rigid position.

All was now ready — and the two semi-trailers moved off, slowly followed by the Lancaster. The tail of the convoy consisted of the big mobile crane and two service vehicles. We used the back roads on the airport and at times it was necessary for the aircraft to traverse the lawns in order to get around a bend. In order to get on to the tarmac area we had to pass through some newly-built fence gates. Staff of the Department of Transport had removed a section of the fence to allow the aircraft to pass. Unfortunately, the aircraft did not clear some of the fence posts. A concerted effort (despite the pouring rain) was made to remove these posts but they were set in concrete and would not budge. In desperation we called up our mobile crane, which made short work of the posts — pulling them clean out of the ground!

Resuming our transit of the airport, we were met by the Department of Transport vehicle that would lead us across the main runway. These vehicles have two-way radio sets and are in constant touch with the control tower. We could hear the Tower giving instructions that our convoy had to wait until a South African Airways Boeing 747 had landed. The airliner eventually landed and while it was taxying to the terminal apron, we overheard part of the conversation between the Tower and the captain of

Above left: **The convoy reaches the boundary of the airport by the end of the main runway.**

Left: **A view of the road procession showing the width to which the Lancaster's span was cut down.**

Above: **Newly on site next to the Aviation Museum, the Lancaster's port wing is being lowered into place.**

the 747, which must have followed an enquiry from the latter. 'The aircraft you see now entering the main runway,' reported the Tower, 'is the model to be used on tourist flights to South Africa!' The 747 captain acknowledged the call without further comment having been either none too pleased by this remark or too busy with the ground handling of his aircraft.

After the Tower gave us the 'all clear', our convoy moved onto the runway and started out towards the end of the field. At 5mph it was quite amazing how long it took before we reached the airport's boundary fence. A section of this fence had been removed to allow the aircraft to pass and so we came to what is known as the 'crash-road'. This was the road which eventually brought us to the highway. By then, it was 17.00hrs and we parked for the night on the crash road. The Author, in his 'pilot'-vehicle, stayed overnight with the aircraft — just in case. Although the vehicle carried sleeping accommodation, I did not get much sleep because at various intervals during the

night, either an airport crash tender or a security van passed by on the boundary patrol and used their spotlights to find out what sort of a contraption was standing outside the fence. As the rain was coming down in buckets, I felt loath to leave the car and furnish the information!

The second part of the journey began at 06.00hrs on Sunday 19 August 1979. The rain had stopped but it was bitterly cold. After 'breakfast', we checked the Lancaster's wheels and turntable and made a general inspection of all the vehicles and their loads. By 07.00hrs, two motor vehicles and three motorcycles from the Police Traffic Department arrived. Morning 'cuppa' was duly served and much appreciated after which the convoy got underway leaving the 'crash-road' and entering the main highway. The Mains Roads Department was also present, probably just to make sure the aircraft did not knock down any of their traffic lights. However, the whole journey of 16 miles went without a hitch. At times the 24ft wide 'Lanc' had to straddle the islands in the middle of the highway, but otherwise the trip caused no problems and by 08.30hrs the convoy had arrived at the AFA Estate. The aircraft was placed on prepared concrete hardstands and with the help of the crane, which Bellway Pty allowed us to use a little longer, both wings were put back on the aircraft by 11.00hrs.

In the course of the following weeks, we mounted both the outer engines, props and elevators. The aircraft is being worked on constantly and particular attention is given to the rust-proofing of all metal and parts. In due course, the machine — currently parked next to our Aviation Museum — will be completely repainted.

That, then, was the story of the Lancaster 'shift', but what of the AFA Aviation Museum itself.

Like any other Group involved with aviation history, ours has been a battle for many years. It has been dedication and enthusiasm which kept our 45 members going. We had the scantiest of work facilities and no space for storage. A lot of gear was kept in the garages of our members. Generally, funds were very meagre but money was raised by means of social functions or booksales. Many members have deliberately refrained from passing to the Treasurer their bills for various purchases of equipment, etc. Trips to the 'bush' in our own vehicles in order to collect some engine or other part were often considered 'a day's outing' and we paid for the petrol ourselves. Perhaps I ought to remind the readers that when one speaks in this country of going to the 'bush', this might well entail travelling for hundreds of miles!

Probably one of the reasons for our low membership numbers has been the fact that no proper workshop was available. However, this situation has now been remedied and we expect more people to join the Group. In order to acquaint the public of our existence, our Committee decided early in 1978 to organise an exhibition. With the co-operation of a very large supermarket in one of Perth's suburbs, we 'borrowed' part of their below-ground parking area. The Group spent a great deal of effort on this project and it was very rewarding to have our State Governor, Air Marshal Sir Wallace Kyle, open the exhibition. This show, in which various airlines also took part, lasted for 14 days. It was a great success and thousands of people came to see it. Financially we came out even but we were way ahead in terms of the publicity we received.

During 1979, the State of Western Australia celebrated its 150th anniversary. The Industry Committee of the body organising the anniversary, WAY '79, raised $100,000; and in order to have a permanent reminder of the State's 150th year, it was decided to grant this money to the Air Force Association to enable them to erect a Museum. Construction of the building was started in May 1979 and completed in early-August; the building has a floor area of 1,250m² and its hyperbolic parabola roof has created a lot of attention. The roof is self-supporting and does not require internal columns, thus leaving a clear space for the exhibits. For our purpose, this was a very important design feature, particularly so when moving aircraft around.

The opening was planned for the middle of November 1979, leaving the Group about three months to get all the exhibits ready. As one might well imagine, however, many other things besides the actual exhibits, were needed — fixtures, stands, display boards, etc — in addition to the actual exhibits. Bearing in mind that most of our members had to earn their daily living between 08.00-17.00hrs, the preparations involved a lot of work during the evenings.

In the yards of the Government Railways, two former railway station kiosks were located — one in bits and pieces and the other in a reasonable state. The latter was completely reconditioned by Mr A. Buzza, who also carried out the complete rebuild of the Museum's Moth Minor. In both cases he did a splendid job. The reconditioned kiosk now serves as our souvenir shop and it is the location of some brisk and very welcome trade. The bits and pieces of the other kiosk consisted mainly of some timber and a

quantity of veneered panelling. These were refurbished and used for display boards — nothing was wasted! In time for the opening, we also received on loan an 80kg chunk of Skylab which had fallen in the bush country of south western 'WA' after its much publicised descent from Earth orbit.

Finally, on 17 November, in the presence of many guests, members of parliament and the Industry Committee WAY '79, the Museum was officially opened by Capt Cyril Kleinig, OA, the retired director of MacRobertson Airlines (now Ansett Airlines). The guest of honour was the West Australian aviation pioneer, Sir Norman Brearley. After the opening, the guests were conducted through the Museum by the Honorary Curator, Mr Frank Purser.

Since the establishment of the Museum, public attendance and support has been extremely good. We

Below left: An artist's impression of the Museum building with the Lancaster in the adjoining enclosure.

Above right: An interior view of the Museum during its construction, showing the specially designed roof permitting a clear floor display area.

Right: The shop kiosk, with its selection of souvenirs.

Below: Some of the Museum exhibits — Commonwealth Wackett, Vampire T11 and Moth Minor.

have found that many schools also regard visits to the Museum of great educational value. While on a 'flying' visit to Perth in December 1979, Gp Capt Sir Douglas Bader honoured us with a visit.

The smaller display items in the Museum are regularly rotated but on permanent exhibit are the Lancaster, Spitfire, de Havilland Moth Minor, Commonwealth Wirraway and Wackett, Heath Parasol (also rebuilt by Mr Buzza), de Havilland Vampire and a Demoiselle replica which was specially built for the film *Those Magnificent Men in their Flying Machines* — the latter machine has been on loan from Ansett Airlines.

The Group has about 50 aircraft engines, ranging from a working nine-cylinder Le Rhone rotary to a Rolls Royce Dart turboprop. Also on display is a massive 18-cylinder Wright Turbo-Compound which originally came from a Super Constellation used by NASA.

In our Workshop we still have various engines under repair. One, in particular, is being specially prepared 'as is'. The well-corroded relic was recovered from Broome harbour and belonged to an American Fortress which was shot down by the Japanese during the 1942 air raid on Broome. The remains of this B-17 can still be seen at low tide.

Being restored for static display are an Auster, Tiger Moth, Avro Anson and a Mustang. All these

Below: **Some of the Museum's powerplant display — jet engines and a Wright turbo-compound piston engine from a Super Constellation. The large canvas in the background portrays a Flying Doctor Service scene.**

are long term projects and will require an enormous amount of work and time but I am certain that the work will be completed. The RAAF recently phased out that famous aircraft, the Douglas DC-3, and rumour has it that one has been allocated to the WA Air Force Association. If this is correct, we will indeed be indebted to Air Marshal Sir Wallace Kyle.

In 1979 a special appeal fund was launched to enable the Group to build a roof over the Lancaster. Although this Appeal is well on the way, a lot more finance is required before the building can be started. The Group has been trying very hard to obtain some portable classrooms that have become available. If our endeavours are successful, one of these will be used to house our library and archives. The documentary collection is under the direction of Mr M. Prime, our research officer and official photographer — most of the accompanying photographs are his work.

New ideas and suggestions for the development of the Museum are constantly put forward. Sometimes these thoughts can be put into action immediately but often they have to wait for various reasons. As most aviation historical groups well know, restoration and all that goes with it is a slow and laborious task.

I hope that the foregoing will provide an impression of the aircraft preservation activity in Western Australia. The Aviation Historical Group of the State's AFA Branch is dedicated to continuing with the task in hand and while much has been achieved, it is recognised that there is also much still to be done; fortunately, the Group has benefitted from a totally committed membership — long may its perseverance continue unabated.

The Royal Jordanian 'FALCONS'

T.M. ENGLISH

A WELCOME SIGHT at many of the European air displays during the past two years has been the Royal Jordanian Falcons aerobatic team. Flying the diminutive Pitts S-2A Special, the Royal Falcons gave their first European display at the 1979 Paris Salon. This and the Greenham Common International Air Tatto were the only European displays scheduled for their 1979 display season. However, such was their popularity that by the end of September 1979 they had appeared at no less than 43 shows and are currently (September 1980) coming to the end of a 3½ month display tour in the UK.

The Royal Falcons were formed in 1978 with the principal aim of promoting Jordan and ALIA — the Jordanian national airline and the team's sponsor. A secondary aim is to increase the awareness of aviation within Jordan. All of the team are civilians, including Capt Paul Warsaw, the Director of Operations. The founder members of the team, Hani Zumot and Jalal Katiab, received their initial training in the USA from Paul Warsaw. In addition to his role as Director of

Above: **The Royal Falcons making smoke in vic-three formation with JY-RJJ in the lead, JY-RJH on the port wing and JY-RJG to starboard.**
T. M. English

Operations, Paul is joint owner of an aerobatic training school in Fort Lauderdale, Fl. Final training was carried out at the team's home base, Amman airport.

When the team first flew at Amman, onlookers were apparently frightened at the sight of the gyrating Pitts. The manoeuvres were completely foreign to the general run of airliner traffic to and from the airport. However, it was not long before some of the regular spectators were making sensible criticism of the manoeuvres — an indication that the secondary aim of the team was being realised.

Above: **The members of the Royal Falcons aerobatic team. From left to right, Hani Zumot (lead, flies JY-RJJ), Jalal Katiab (No 3 in JY-RJH) and Adnan Takruri (No 2 in JY-RJG).**

Right: **The team in echelon over Bough Beech reservoir, southeast of Biggin Hill with JY-RJJ emitting puffs of smoke.** *T. M. English*

Building on the success of their 1979 season, a third Pitts S-2A, JY-RJJ, was added to the existing pair, JY-RJG and JY-RJH. The third aircraft, flown by Adnan Takruri, enabled the team to vary the repertoire for their 1980 displays. It is still a relatively small team, however, and they wisely fly 'low-energy' manoeuvres. This enables them to perform continuously within a tight box. 'High energy' manoeuvres require breaks in the display for aircraft to regain energy lost in manoeuvres. With a larger team this is not a problem; an element can perform 'fill-in' manoeuvres, like the Red Arrow's synchro-pair.

The Royal Falcons intend to expand still further and have a fourth Pitts S-2A currently in reserve. It will be flown by Hussein Al-Subuh who is co-pilot of the team's support aircraft, a BN Islander, JY-DCA. Before flying a four-ship formation, though, the Royal Falcons are going to increase their experience with three aircraft. The team are also hoping to replace their Pitts S-2As with S-2S versions in time for the 1981 display season. Powered by a 260hp engine, compared with the 200hp of the S-2A, it will have a greatly improved vertical performance. It also has symmetrical ailerons which double the maximum roll rate.

In addition to flying, the three pilots are responsible for the maintenance of their aircraft. In this respect, the Royal Falcons are autonomous; Paul has an A1 authorisation (Jordanian rating) and Hani has a powerplant/airframe engineers licence. As if this didn't keep them occupied they all have secondary duties. Paul is captain of the Islander and continues to instruct and advise the team; Hani is responsible for overall maintenance; Adnan for administration and Jalal for logistics.

Above: **Hani Zumot leads with JY-RJJ inverted and Jalal Katiab and Adnan Takruri on the port and starboard wings respectively.**

Top right: **A close-up view of the Pitts S-2A, JY-RJJ, formating with the camera aircraft, the team's support BN Islander.** *Both: T. M. English*

Right: **The Islander, JY-DCA at Hurn for the Bournemouth Air Pageant.** *Daniel March*

ALIA provide financial support to the Royal Falcons and also assist in transportation. A Boeing 707 belonging to the airline is used to airlift the Pitts to and from Jordan at the beginning and end of the display seasons. Instrumental in the establishment of the team, however, was King Hussein — hence the 'Royal' prefix. A well known and capable pilot in his own right, King Hussein is also reputed to be the Royal Falcons keenest supporter. The Royal Jordanian Falcons are currently the only aerobatic team in the Middle East and may soon be the only professional civilian aerobatic team to be seen in Europe. Long may they reign!

106

The Boeing B-52
STRATOFORTRESS

KARL E. HAYES and EAMON C. POWER

Below: **Boeing B-52D Stratofortress of the 22nd Bomb Wing on landing roll at March AFB, Ca with braking parachute, spoilers and flaps deployed.**
F. B. Mormillo

IN 1946, the world had just come through the terrible holocaust of World War 2. The United States, having learned the extreme value of a long-range bomber force, was in the process of establishing the Strategic Air Command to organise such a capability within what was to become the USAF. A preliminary design contract was awarded to the Boeing company in June of that year for a long-range heavy bomber powered by turboprop engines. It seems incredible that the aircraft which emerged from that design contract is still an essential front-line bomber, and likely to remain so into the foreseeable future.

The aircraft in question is, of course, the Boeing B-52 Stratofortress. It started out as a six engine turboprop design with straight wings, but in October 1948 Boeing submitted an entirely new proposal, the Model 464, which embodied the basic B-52 configuration as we know it today. There were two prototypes, designated XB-52 and YB-52, the latter being the first to fly on 15 April 1952. The most radical difference between these prototypes and the production versions was the tandem cockpit arrangement of the former, whereas the production models have more conventional airliner-type flightdecks with side-by-side seating.

B-52 variants

The first example of the initial production version, the B-52A, first flew on 5 August 1954. Only three test A models were produced, the true production variant being the essentially similar B-52B, which had a 37,700 USgall fuel capacity (including a 1,000 USgall auxiliary tank under each outboard wing). A total of 50 B model aircraft were built, of which 27 were RB-52Bs with reconnaissance capability. The B-52B was powered by eight Pratt & Whitney J57-19W engines and had a maximum gross weight of 360,000lb. The first Stratofortress to be delivered to SAC, namely B-52B s/n 52-8711, which joined the 93rd Bomb Wing at Castle AFB, Ca in June 1955 has been preserved, and now resides peacefully in the SAC Museum at Offutt AFB, Nb. The B-52C featured 3,000 USgall underwing tanks and a 410,000lb gross weight; like the B model, it was available in B-52C bomber or RB-52C reconnaissance variants. In all, 35 Cs were built. The B-52D was essentially similar to the C model, although it had no reconnaissance capability. One hundred and seventy Ds were built, and all were later given 'Big Belly' modifications which increased their conventional bomb carrying capability. The B-52E differed only slightly from the D, incorporating various changes in the bombing, navigation and electronics systems. As well as pioneering the use of the AGM-28 Hound Dog supersonic nuclear armed missile, the E model was also used to develop the low altitude penetration techniques which have been a significant feature of SAC's battle plans since the late-1950s. The E model held the distinction of being the cheapest of all B-52s, at just under $6million per copy. One hundred E models were built. The F model was similar to its immediate predecessors, but had uprated J57-P-43W engines that were also to power the G model. Eighty nine Fs were built.

The next B-52 variant, the G model, differed radically from its predecessors. The lofty, pointed tail which towered 48ft from the ground was cropped to

Below: **Two views of 22nd Bomb Wing B-52Ds in the flightline area at March AFB; the aircraft are s/nos 56-0592 (upper photo) and 56-0629.** *All photos in this article by Eamon C. Power, unless otherwise credited*

Above: **A threequarter-rear view of a B-52G, s/n 59-2584, of the 2nd Bomb Wing during landing approach. Note the sizeable inboard and outboard flap areas and the spoiler just visible above the starboard wing.**

40ft, and the tail gunner's position was replaced by a remotely controlled, radar-equipped unit. The internal fuel capacity was greatly increased to 46,000 USgall, to which was added 1,400 USgall from two reduced size underwing tanks. Various other detail improvements were included in the B-52G, including underwing pylons for the carriage of Hound Dog missiles. A total of 193 B-52Gs was built. The final version, the B-52H, was essentially similar to the G model except that the 'straight jet' J57 engines were replaced by Pratt & Whitney TF-33 turbofans, which bestowed valuable payload/range performance improvements, and the machine guns in the tail were replaced with a single Vulcan cannon. The performance improvements were highlighted by two records established in the early-1960s — a 12,532 statute mile straight line record between Kadena, Japan, and Torrejon, Spain, on 10-11 January 1962 and an 11,336 statute mile closed circuit record on 6-7 June 1962. A total of 102 B-52Hs was built, the final example being delivered to SAC on 22 June 1962. In all, including the two prototypes and three test aircraft, 744 B-52s in 8 different variants were built over a 10-year period.

Even before the last of the B-52s came off the line, a proposed successor was on the way — the North American XB-70 Valkyrie. The XB-70 was a six-engined Mach 3 delta design, but its substantial development costs led to its relegation to a research project in 1964. A second attempt was made ten years later in the shape of the Rockwell B-1, which was a slightly less ambitious design in terms of size and performance (Mach 2.2), but was nonetheless a very technologically advanced design incorporating variable geometry reminiscent of Boeing's initial SST proposals. The first B-1 flew on 13 December 1974, and about $4 billion had been spent or committed to the project when President Carter cancelled it in June 1977. At that time, the US Defense Secretary, Harold Brown, explained that the requirement for the B-1 was obviated by the cruise missile, which could be launched from the B-52 outside the Soviet defence system.

The United States' strategic forces comprise three basic elements, collectively known as the Triad — land based intercontinental ballistic missiles, Navy submarine-launched ballistic missiles and long range manned bomber aircraft. The B-52 constitutes the major part of the bomber element of Triad, as it has done since the late-1950s. The manned bombers are

the most flexible element of Triad. They can be launched to demonstrate National resolve, as well as during periods of heightened international tension. Being under positive control, they can (unlike missiles) be recalled if the situation dictates. Manned bombers are not committed to a predetermined course and can readily adjust to the changing conditions of a combat situation. These bombers are also an integral part of the SAC Alert Force. The requirement for such a force arises from the need to be able to react to a situation within the available warning time. Given the devastating power of nuclear weapons and the speed of modern delivery systems, a nation can be disabled in a matter of hours. Technological advances have allowed Soviet ICBMs to be but 30 minutes from United States cities and Soviet intermediate range ballistic missiles and attack aircraft a few minutes away from western Europe. SAC's answer to this problem is the Alert Force, which was instituted on 1 October 1957 when a number of SAC aircraft went on airborne alert; the latter programme ended the following year, and was replaced by a 24 hour/day ground alert, ready to react well within the warning time provided by attack warning systems.

Most SAC bases have alert facilities. These are high security areas, situated away from the main base area, where a number of bombers and KC-135 tankers are parked, fully fuelled and armed and ready for immediate launch. The facilities include living quarters for the crews, where they must spend their

Above: **A B-52H, s/n 60-0058, of the 410th Bomb Wing on landing finals.**

Above right: **A view from the control tower of the flightline area at Castle AFB, Ca showing B-52Fs (since withdrawn) and KC-135s of the 93rd Bomb Wing.**

alert duty, usually one week in three. Although somewhat arduous, the Alert Force vastly increases the value and effectiveness of SAC's nuclear deterrent.

The B-52 (together with SAC's only other manned bomber, the FB-111) has therefore a vital role to play, and progressive modifications have ensured that it remains a viable weapons system. During the latter half of the 1960s, the B-52Bs, Cs and Es were progressively withdrawn, and the B-52F relegated to the training role. By the end of 1978 the remaining B-52Fs had also been withdrawn to the storage compounds at Davis-Monthan AFB. This left the B-52D, G and H in front-line service.

B-52 modernization efforts have not been limited to the nuclear role, and expanding Soviet/Warsaw Pact conventional war-fighting capabilities have resulted in an increased emphasis on the B-52's conventional role. This role has fallen for the most part on the B-52D. Although many of the Ds have been withdrawn, 80 of the best aircraft were retained, and subjected to the 'Pacer Plank' programme during

1975-77, under which a new wing was fitted, thus extending the service life by about 7,000 hours. All are 'Big Belly' aircraft, with a weapon load of 54,000lb. The primary missions of the D model are now seen as tactical bombing with conventional bombs and anti-shipping operations in which mines, TV-guided glide bombs or laser-guided bombs are used. These roles are reflected in the colour-scheme — suitable for night bombing missions: black under surfaces, fuselage sides and tail, with camouflaged upper surfaces. (The G and H models have white heat reflective undersides in keeping with their primary nuclear strike role.) The Pacer Plank modifications became necessary as by 1973 significant structural cracks had appeared in the wings, attributed in part to operations in Southeast Asia. The modifications cost a reported $2.6million per aircraft, but it should be remembered that 1971 was the original phase-out date for the D model, which can now continue to perform these vital tasks well into the 1980s. The D model also retains its nuclear capability.

The backbone of the nuclear bomber force consists of about 250 B-52G and H models. Over the last few years, a number of concurrent modernization programmes have been undertaken on these aircraft, which have greatly increased their effectiveness. These programmes can be summarised as follows:

(1) Cartridge starters have been fitted to the J57 turbojets of the B-52G and to the TF-33 turbofan engines of the B-52H, enabling an immediate and simultaneous start of all 8 engines, thereby reducing reaction time by 2 minutes, a very important factor in an attack situation.

(2) An electro-optical viewing system (EVS) comprising two nose-mounted steerable turrets containing a Hughes AAQ-6 forward looking infra-red sensor (starboard) and a Westinghouse AVQ-22 low light television (port). Data from these sensors is presented to the crew via CRT screens in the cockpit. The information comes across as a profile of the terrain ahead of the aircraft, with an artificial horizon to indicate the aircraft's relative position. This equipment permits all-weather low-level penetration missions. Additional information such as airspeed, and time to weapons release also appears on the screen.

(3) Phase 6 ECM package, designed to provide greater protection in high-threat areas. Included are a jammer unit to confuse enemy radars and carriage of double the previous number of infra-red deceiving flares.

(4) Short Range Attack Missile (SRAM) launchers have been installed at a cost of some $359million. Structural changes involved repositioned hardpoints in the aft bomb bay for the 8-missile rotary launcher. An additional 12 missiles are carried under wing, six per side. The missile, a replacement of the Hound Dog and designated AGM-69A is over 14ft long, weighs nearly 2,000lb and has a speed of Mach 2.5 over a maximum range of 100 miles. In addition to the 20 SRAMs, the B-52G/H can carry 4 gravity bombs in the weapons bay, further enhancing attack flexibility.

113

Above: **A B-52D on approach to March AFB, Ca; note the large underwing tanks, ECM antennae aft of the rear main gear and the classic skin wrinkling on the fuselage side.**

Centre right: **Tail turret on a B-52D.** *Frank B. Mormillo*

Bottom right: **Detail shot of a landing B-52H of the 319th Bomb Wing; note the antennae forward and aft of the main gear units, the weapons pylon attachments inboard of the inner engines, the open ports on the low light level TV and forward-looking infra-red pods below the cockpit and the fact that the No 5 engine is not under power (the intake blow-in doors are closed).**

Wurtsmith AFB

The Authors recently visited a typical SAC alert base, and were afforded a close look at the B-52 operation. Wurtsmith AFB in Michigan has had long connections with the B-52, and was an appropriate location to see the aircraft at work. The base is named after a famous Detroit aviator, Major General Paul Wurtsmith who had a distinguished career in action in World War 2, and is located 3 miles northwest of the town of Oscoda, on the shores of Lake Huron and about 160 miles north of Detroit. The base was originally called Camp Skeel, and was used from the mid-twenties as a gunnery camp for Selfridge Field. It was later re-named Oscoda Army Air Field, and was used during WW2 for training Free French pilots. After the war it became a fighter base, being the home of the 412th Fighter Group, which remained until April 1960, at which stage the base was signed over to SAC.

The host unit at Wurtsmith is the 379th Bomb Wing, which was activated on 1 November 1955. Training began with the delivery of its first aircraft, a B-47, on 20 April 1956, the Wing then being located at Homestead AFB, Fl. On 20 February 1960, Headquarters USAF announced that the 379th BW was to convert to B-52s in 1961, and in fact the last B-47 assigned to the Wing left Homestead on 21 December 1960. Coincidental with the change to the B-52, the 379th also moved north to Wurtsmith, and became the first unit to receive the ultimate B-52 version, the B-52H, taking delivery of its first aircraft on 9 May 1961. A major reshuffle occurred in June 1977, when the 379th BW exchanged its B-52Hs with the B-52Gs operated by the 28th BW at Ellsworth AFB, South Dakota, and from that date to the present, the 379th has flown the G model.

The Wing was under the command of Colonel Jesse S. Hocker at the time of our visit. Col Hocker has had a distinguished career in the USAF since he joined on

19 December 1954. He has seen active duty in Southeast Asia, and has 205 combat missions in the F-4 and 22 in the B-52 to his credit. His decorations and awards include the Distinguished Flying Cross, the Meritorious Service Medal with Oak Leaf cluster, the Air Medal with 12 Oak Leaf clusters and the Air Force Commendation Medal. We were accorded the privilege of an interview with Col Hocker, who in addition spared some of his time to see us off on our KC-135 mission and to meet us after the mission to ensure all went well.

There are two aircraft operating squadrons under the 379th BW at Wurtsmith — the 524th Bomb Squadron, with the B-52Gs, and the 920th Air Refueling Squadron, with the KC-135As. In addition, there is also a small unit of Cessna T-37s assigned to Wurtsmith as part of the Accelerated Co-pilot Enrichment (ACE) Program, to provide co-pilots with the necessary flying experience without incurring the major expense of flying B-52s or KC-135s. These T-37s are drawn from the 71st FTW at Vance AFB, Ok.

Wurtsmith is also the home of the 40th Air Division, the unit which supervises and monitors the operation of the 379th BW at Wurtsmith, as well as the 410th BW at K.I. Sawyer AFB, Mi, the 305th Air Refueling Wing at Grissom AFB, In, and the 351st Strategic Missile Wing at Whiteman AFB, Mo. In addition, the 40th AD acts as advisor to three Aerial Reserve Force units — the 126th ARW of the Illinois ANG at O'Hare International Airport, the 128th Air

Below: **A wet day at Wurtsmith AFB, Mi with a 379th Bomb Wing B-52G and its reflections on the ramp.**

Refueling Group of the Wisconsin ANG at General Billy Mitchell Field, and the 931st ARG, AFRES, at Grissom AFB, all flying the KC-135. The 40th AD is one of four such Divisions which comprise SAC's Eighth Air Force, headquartered at Barksdale AFB, La and which is broadly responsible for SAC units in the eastern half of the United States.

Maintenance programme

With fairly elderly B-52Gs and KC-135As, the maintenance organisation plays a particularly important role in maintaining an adequate level of preparedness at a front-line alert base such as Wurtsmith. Both aircraft types have now gone well over the maximum lives originally envisaged, and while extensive update and modification programmes have been undertaken, the basic engine/airframe combination is still the original. A factor which eases the task of maintaining such elderly machines is the general acknowledgement of Boeing's support service as being second to none, a fact to which most airlines can readily testify (and indeed we found the maintenance personnel at Wurtsmith to be of similar outlook). In addition, the J-57 powerplant, which is common to both the B-52G and the KC-135, is basically a very reliable engine, even though it is of 1940s design, and has been in service in one form or another since 1953. It is, of course, basically similar to the commercial JT3C-6, which saw widespread use in early versions of the Boeing 707 and DC-8.

In common with most USAF bases, there are four maintenance squadrons directly involved in the technical support of the B-52s and KC-135s. Wurtsmith has the capability of undertaking virtually all regular maintenance on the assigned fleet with the exception of the major inspections, which are carried out at various specialist locations. Consequently, the maintenance facility is comprehensively equipped with all necessary overhaul shops and test equipment needed to support the 32 strong aircraft inventory, the sophisticated B-52 avionics requiring particularly specialised facilities.

Most of the maintenance functions are undertaken by four maintenance squadrons — the 379th Avionics Maintenance Squadron (AMS), the 379th Field Maintenance Squadron (FMS), the 379th Munitions Maintenance Squadron (MMS) and the 379th Organizational Maintenance Squadron (OMS). These all report to the Wing's Deputy Commander for Maintenance. The 379th AMS, as its name implies, is responsible for the avionics systems on the aircraft. In addition to the normal navigation and communications equipment, the unit also handles the bombing and defensive equipment systems on the B-52. The radar controlled gun systems are checked out in a sophisticated test rig which can duplicate the

radar target of a trailing hostile aircraft. Another rig enables the EVS to be checked out, providing realistic test displays for the pilot's cockpit display. We were also shown how recent technological advances in avionics have led to dramatic reductions in the size of on-board equipment. Apart from the reduced space needed, the newer equipment weighs far less and has superior reliabiity, a particularly impressive comparison being the HF communications transceiver.

The 379th FMS is the largest of the maintenance squadrons, and embodies five branches, each with specific areas of responsibility. These cover such functions as major airframe, aircraft systems (such as pressurisation, fuel, hydraulics, flight controls etc) ground equipment and engines.

The 379th MMS is responsible for the weapons release systems, for the loading, removal and storage of the weapons themselves, and for the associated support equipment. A specialist unit is responsible for the handling of the SRAM missiles.

Finally, the 379th OMS is responsible for the various line maintenance functions, such as pre and post flight inspections, minor defect rectification, replenishment of fuel and oxygen supplies and the provision of ground power and compressed air equipment. In addition, there are various ancillary support units which carry out sundry other support tasks on the base. In all, there are about 11,000 people on base at Wurtsmith.

The aircraft are maintained on a progressive maintenance schedule, with service checks being performed after every 100 flying hours, a full phase being completed after 600 hours. The aircraft go for a major overhaul — called Program Depot Maintenance (PDM) — after every 2,000 hours, or roughly 3 years, which involves major structural inspection, component replacement, repaint, and modification update where necessary. At the time of our visit, one bomber and one tanker were away on PDM. The engines are subjected to hot-end inspections after every 1,600 hours, this work being performed in the shops at Wurtsmith. After every 4,000 hours they are sent to depot for major overhaul. The USAF employs a careful engine monitoring programme whereby crews take a series of readings at various power settings on every flight; these are subsequently analysed by maintenance technicians so that any departure from the engine's 'signature', as established during ground running after overhaul, can be quickly established. Any abnormal trend — such as suddenly increased turbine temperatures, or low-running RPM — can often point to impending trouble, in which case the engine is replaced before further, more serious, problems occur. The in-flight performance monitoring is also backed up by advanced oil analysis. Wurtsmith's dedicated maintenance people have reason to be proud of their low engine in-flight shut-down rate of 1 per 4,000 flying hours on the combined B-52/KC-135 fleet.

Wurtsmith's maintenance personnel have developed a highly efficient Job Control Center (JCC) to maximise aircraft serviceability and optimise the use of available manpower. The system is fully computerised, and is designed to enable the maintenance planning personnel to take rapid and effective decisions so as to ensure maximum aircraft availability. The JCC includes a large status board showing the maintenance status of all assigned aircraft, and computer displays enable additional data such as spares stocks and work schedules to be called up. The Center has a comprehensive communications facility with the various line maintenance organisations and also with the aircraft themselves. A B-52 or KC-135 returning from a mission calls the centre with full data on the aircraft's serviceability status so that appropriate action can be taken as soon as possible. In many cases, defect rectification action may already be in progress even before the aircraft arrives. The Job Control Center at Wurtsmith has proved to be such a success that its design has been adopted by other SAC bases.

There are always B-52s and KC-135s on the alert pad at Wurtsmith, fuelled, armed and ready to go. Practice alerts are regularly staged, but they never progress beyond the end of the runway, since aircraft are not flown with nuclear ordnance unless absolutely necessary. The aircraft undergo pre-flight inspections daily, during which some defects might be highlighted; the practice alerts also provide further opportunities to check out the serviceability of systems. However, it is obviously impossible to fully assess the aircraft's serviceability unless a full mission profile is flown, and consequently the FSAGA (First Sortie After Ground Alert) has become a vital part of the maintenance function in relation to Alert aircraft. After spending 89 days on alert, a B-52 has its nuclear weapon removed, and is then scheduled on a routine training mission. No maintenance other than routine pre-flight work is performed, and particular attention is devoted during the mission to checking out all systems on board. In this way, it is possible to determine how well the aircraft would have performed if a real alert had taken place. The performance of B-52s on FSAGA is very carefully monitored by the maintenance personnel, and should any undesirable trends emerge, appropriate action will be taken, which could be, for example, to reduce the period spent on alert.

From the flying aspect, the base is located in fairly ideal terrain. The runway is 11,800ft long and 300ft wide, and operations are normally conducted, wind permitting, in a westerly direction, which puts the approaches over Lake Huron. To the west of the base is Alpena State Forest, which at the time of our visit in the autumn presented a very spectacular backdrop of yellows, oranges and reds, particularly when viewed from the air. Wurtsmith gets warm, pleasant weather during the summer, as evidenced by the many resorts which line the shores of the lake, but winters can be quite severe, with fronts frequently coming down from Canada.

Training mission

Contrary to opinion in some quarters, SAC exists on a very tight budget, and flying on the expensive B-52 has to be kept to a minimum consistent with maintaining adequate levels of crew proficiency. Apart from the inexorably rising cost of JP4 fuel (the non-fan B-52G burns about 4,000 USgall/hour), the need to conserve airframe life is also vital, bearing in mind that there is still no certainty of a successor in the foreseeable future. Consequently, the very maximum has to be obtained from each training mission, and as many tasks as possible are scheduled during a typical 6-8 hr sortie. We sat in on a briefing for a detail which included a low level bomb run and a refuelling from a KC-135 which we would accompany.

The B-52 was commanded by Captain John Pitstick, and he and his five crewmembers painstakingly went through each of their roles for our benefit during the mission briefing. The mission was to consist of a departure from Wurtsmith and a routing out to the north to establish on a westerly heading to converge with the tanker. After transferring a nominal amount of fuel, several additional dry hook-ups were to be performed so as to give both aircraft commander (AC) and co-pilot experience at this demanding task. The entire exercise was to be performed on a linear refuelling track starting over Lake Michigan and running across the States of Wisconsin, Minnesota and North Dakota. This is in contrast to the racetrack patterns which have to be employed in the congested airspace over central Europe. On completion of the air refuelling, the B-52 was to fly north to the Canadian border where a U-turn pattern would be flown, descending to fly a low-level route to a simulated target — in fact, some unsuspecting farmer's grain silo located near Bismark, ND. The U-turn pattern is called a trombone entry, the length of the manoeuvre being varied to allow for fine adjustment of the schedule, since the time on target is normally held to ±2½ minutes. Three runs were planned on the target — two conventional bomb runs and one SRAM attack. The low-level route is one of several clearly defined runs in the Continental United States

Above: **'Boy 24', the 379th BW B-52G, s/n 58-0185, positioned astern of the KC-135 tanker, call-sign 'Polio 50',**

(CONUS), and times of usage are promulgated, not only to warn off other airspace users, but also to advise any citizens who might be in the path of the impressive but somewhat startling sight of a massive B-52 hurtling along at 1,000 feet or less. To minimise public inconvenience, tracks are over sparsely populated terrain, with a minimum height of 400 feet, at subsonic speeds. The total length of time from entry to exit on this low level route is about 45 minutes, and bombing accuracy is established by a ground based radar bomb scoring site. Radar bomb scoring began in 1946 and replaced the initial primitive methods of dropping sand bags or dummy bombs on circles drawn on the ground. The electronic equipment is operated and maintained by SAC technicians located at Strategic Training Range (STR) detachments, consisting of mobile buildings and trailers. Using a combination of radio and radar contact between aircraft and the STR site, the effectiveness of combat crews is scored without having to drop bombs. In fact, bombs are not carried on these training missions. Bomb scoring radars 'lock

on' the approaching bomber, tracking it automatically on a plotting board. Just before the simulated release of the bomb, the aircraft transmits a tone to the STR site by radio. The point of simulated bomb release is indicated by stopping the tone. By using figures of distance, direction, ground speed, heading, altitude, wind conditions, bomb fall characteristics and other data, STR technicians compute the accuracy of the particular mission. They can determine if the target was hit, and if not, by how far and in what direction it was missed. Low-level exercises are an important part of B-52 training since the aircraft's penetration capability is now largely based on such profiles, a radically different role to that originally envisaged for the high altitude bomber. On completion of the bomb runs, the B-52 would climb back to altitude for recovery back to Wurtsmith, where some circuit work would be undertaken prior to the final landing.

The B-52G has a crew of six — two pilots, an electronics warfare officer (EWO), tail gunner, navigator and radar navigator. Interestingly for such a large and complex eight-engined machine, no flight engineer is carried; most of his tasks are undertaken by the co-pilot. The EWO is responsible for monitoring hostile radar transmissions, eg from missile or gun guidance or fighter aircraft control radars which might be directed against the bomber, and must take appropriate action using the B-52's comprehensive ECM equipment. During the simulated exercise, various such 'hostile' radar defences would be directed against the B-52, and the EWO is expected to react accordingly. The tail gunner who sits in the cockpit (in the B-52D he still sits on his own in the rear of the aircraft) has a radar scope showing the situation to the bomber's rear; he also has the gun aiming and firing equipment. The navigator performs the conventional navigation functions, now aided by the versatile inertial navigation system (INS). The radar navigator is responsible for directing the bomb run and the management of the various bombing computers, which can be programmed with the target location (either the target's co-ordinates, or its location with reference to a known waypoint), the aircraft's operating parameters (speed, course, height) and wind factor. It can then either automatically release the bombs, or provide accurate data to the crew for weapons release.

Capt Pitstick was yet another Southeast Asia veteran, having flown Cessna 0-2s in the Forward Air Controller role in Vietnam — a far cry from his current assignment as B-52 aircraft commander! He liked the B-52, and found it a pleasant aircraft to fly. In spite of the radical change in aircraft size, his type conversion to the 8-jet monster took about 8 flying hours, plus extensive simulator time, of course. Indeed, the dedication, enthusiasm and high morale among the B-52 crews was most noticeable, and they are particularly proud of the achievements of the 524th BS, which has twice been awarded Air Force Outstanding Unit Awards. Further evidence of their expertise was the fact that at the 'Giant Voice' bombing competition held in late-November 1979 the 379th BW was awarded the Dougherty SRAM Trophy for the highest score in all simulated SRAM launches. In addition, for the second year running, the 8th Air Force was awarded the Doolittle Trophy for the highest combined average score for B-52 low-level bombing, a record to which the 379th contributed.

One regular task which is not popular with the crews, but which is regarded as a necessary evil is that of the alert duty already referred to. Crews spend roughly one week in three on alert, which involves living, eating and sleeping at the alert facility. The crews may move to certain areas on the base, but a predetermined pick-up plan has to be worked out in the event of an alert. Certain roadways around the main base complex are designated alert routes and are so signposted, and when moving around the base the alert crews use an appropriately placarded Alert Truck to which all other traffic had better give way when it is in a hurry. It is obviously a source of some strain to be in a constant state of no-notice readiness to launch. Practice alerts are regularly staged, often not being called off until the B-52s are on the runway,

ready to roll. It is not until the alert is cancelled that crews know for certain that it is not the real thing.

Wurtsmith now has a full-time B-52 simulator, and the arrival of a KC-135 simulator was imminent at the time of our visit. Hitherto, these simulators were mounted on mobile railcars, and visited the various SAC bases for training details. With the rundown in the number of SAC bases, each remaining base can now have its own simulator full-time. We visited the Wurtsmith facility, which is still installed in a railcar, complete with USAF 'Star-and-Bar' insignia. We were accorded the opportunity to 'fly' the simulator, which provided some concept of the handling qualities of the B-52. While our flying experience on large types is strictly limited, the B-52 felt far heavier and more sluggish than the KC-135. Even when at 16,000ft and 250kts indicated, turns required large control inputs and it took some time for the aircraft to respond; when in the approach configuration, these impressions became even more marked. On the other hand, shut down of even an outboard engine produced remarkably few asymmetric control problems.

We departed on the KC-135 tanker, which was to refuel Capt Pitstick's B-52, some 20 minutes ahead of the receiver. The KC-135 was under the command of Lt-Col Alvarez, who has had a distinguished career in the USAF. Having started out as a navigator on B-57 and B-58 bombers, he underwent pilot training and was assigned onto Lockheed EC-121R Super Constellation electronics intelligence aircraft operating out of Thailand. He then went on to fly Douglas C-118As out of Panama on transport work before being assigned the KC-135. Our call-sign on the mission was 'Polio 50' whilst Capt Pitstick's B-52 was 'Boy 24'. The KC-135 flightline at Wurtsmith is arranged opposite the B-52s, and work was in progress on pre-flighting the two aircraft when we arrived. Our KC-135, s/n 59-1517, was named *Silver Shadow*, and the crew chief confirmed the aircraft fully serviceable and ready to go. We started up ahead of schedule, and after a brief wait at the holding point while a Zantop Electra on a Logair cargo flight landed, we took the active. We were some way below gross take-off weight, so a dry take-off was performed, ie without having to use water injection. Shortly after we became airborne, we heard the receiver taxying for the final external pre-departure check at the runway holding point.

Minneapolis ATC Center handled the vectoring of the B-52, which was at FL260, or 1,000ft below us, and we soon had the aircraft in sight off our starboard, at about 10 miles and closing slowly. This was on 'on course' air-refuelling rendezvous, where tanker and receiver approach from different directions and gradually converge on the one course

over the Air Refuelling Initial Point (ARIP). The other three types of rendezvous are the 'anchor' (where the tanker enters a racetrack pattern and the receiver is vectored towards the tanker to join that pattern — this is the most common type used in Europe), the 'point parallel' (where the receiver is approaching from the opposite direction to the tanker and swings around 180 degrees so as to roll in behind the tanker) and the 'buddy' air refuelling, (where both tanker and receiver depart from the same base and keep company throughout the mission).

We then formally accepted responsibility for separation with the receiver by advising ATC we were 'Going MARSA' — Military Are Responsible for Separation of Aircraft. Boy 24 slid behind us, and began slowly gaining on the 135, drifting upwards. Our boom operator extended the boom, and Capt Pitstick soon had the giant bomber positioned for the contact. Slow closing rates have to be employed, since the B-52 creates quite a bow-wave effect on the tanker's horizontal stabiliser. A successful hook-up was achieved on the first attempt, and fuel transfer began immediately. Unlike fighter aircraft, where control surface movements are barely noticeable, the B-52's ailerons could be seen moving through massive deflections and indeed Capt Pitstick's gloved hand could be seen moving continuously in the B-52 cockpit whilst maintaining station. Such was the level of his skill that the giant bomber remained steadily in position, with only the aileron deflections giving visible evidence of the amount of work required to keep position. On completion of the refuelling, contact was broken, and the bomber retreated for several more practice dry hook-ups. Capt Pitstick then formated off our starboard wing for our benefit,

Above: **A 379th Bomb Wing B-52G, s/n 58-0255, landing at Wurtsmith AFB, Mi.**

before breaking off northwards for the remainder of his exercise.

We turned southwards for a time, and then routed directly back towards Wurtsmith for a celestial navigation exercise. The boom operator took most of the sun-shots via the periscope sextant, and the navigator had a busy time computing positions and advising the AC of course corrections. On arrival at Wurtsmith we performed an orbit exercise, which involves over-flying a given point at a specific time, and flying a 360-degree circuit to arrive back over the start point exactly on a predetermined time. Such an exercise demands very precise work on behalf of the navigator and pilots; one pilot usually concentrates on flying the aircraft, whilst the other handles the throttles, both responding to the commands of the navigator, who has to continually monitor the aircraft's progress through the circle.

Boy 24 was now back in the Wurtsmith area. We descended in for the recovery at Wurtsmith, and flew one practice overshoot before the final landing. The weather had deteriorated during our absence, and it was now raining steadily, although the cloudbase was about 2,500ft with reasonably good visibility underneath. As we taxied back towards the flight line, Boy 24 roared overhead on an overshoot at the start of his 2-hour circuit session.

B-52 features

The B-52's narrow-track 'bicycle' undercarriage configuration and anhedral wing with small tip-to-ground clearance means it is not possible to handle crosswinds in the conventional manner by holding one wing low during the landing. Accordingly, the main gear units can be set from the flightdeck to a predetermined setting computed from the crosswind component so as to permit the aircraft to crab during take off or landing. B-52 pilots say it is disconcerting at first, particularly during landing, where the natural inclination to kick off drift before touchdown has to be consciously suppressed, but evidently one eventually gets used to it. The crosswind gear facility permits operations in crosswinds of up to 30kts.

The B-52's wing is set at a fairly large incidence angle relative to the fuselage. Again because of the bicycle gear layout, the B-52 is not rotated on lift-off like conventional tri-cycle gear aircraft, but flies off in a flat attitude wth a low initial rate of climb on heavy weight take-offs. When the aircraft is light, such as is the case at the end of a mission when performing touch-and-gos, the aircraft lifts off in a marked nose-down attitude, the aft wheels usually becoming airborne first. Flying the pattern, the aircraft maintains a very noticeable nose-down attitude. It is normal practice not to flare the B-52 to any significant extent on touchdown, but rather to let it settle in a flat attitude for simultaneous contact of both main gear units. The outboard spoilers are normally partially deployed during the final stages of the approach, to assist in speed reduction. Thrust reversers are not fitted, and a large braking parachute is deployed to assist in speed reduction on the final full-stop landing.

The wing is of fairly high aspect ratio, and was optimised for the original long-range, high altitude role. Integral fuel tanks are contained in the centre box from root to tip, and the whole structure is quite flexible. When fully fuelled, the outrigger wheels touch the ground; however, when empty, there is a small clearance and the wheels rarely touch the ground at the end of a mission when most of the fuel has been burned off. There are no leading-edge high-lift devices fitted, and the trailing edge flaps are split into two segments on either side with the inboard aileron in between, in classic Boeing configuration. The flap area totals 797ft², and they are simple single-slotted Fowler types unlike the triple-slotted wizardry to which we are now accustomed. Unlike the 707/KC-135, 727 and 747, the B-52 does not have low speed ailerons outboard, but relies on differential spoiler application to augment the inboard ailerons for roll control in extreme situations. Both the rudder and elevators are of surprisingly narrow chord, but the movement arm on such a long fuselage is quite large.

The B-52G's wing span is 185ft, overall length is 160ft 11in and height 40ft 8in. Wing area is about 4,000ft² and sweepback angle is 35 degrees. The maximum all-up weight is 488,000lb and the basic empty weight approximately 200,000lb. Power is provided by eight Pratt & Whitney J57-P-43WB turbojets each rated at 13,750lb static thrust and with water injection capability for high gross weight take-offs. The B-52G has a capacity of 10,000lb of water for this purpose. It is interesting to note that the thrust/weight ratio of the B-52G is considerably lower than that for a current widebody airliner of similar gross weight — eg the 496,000lb TriStar 500, which has 150,000lb total thrust, compared with the B-52G's 110,000 total thrust for a 488,000lb gross weight. However, the turbofan B-52H is quite close to the TriStar 500, having 136,000lb total thrust for a slightly lower 488,000lb gross weight.

Exercises

For SAC to fulfil its role, exercises and combat practice are essential and since 1978, SAC participation in these exercises has been greatly increased (incidentally bringing more B-52 visits to the European theatre). In 'Giant Thrust I', conducted at McConnell AFB, Ks in January 1978, a total of 15 KC-135s operated around the clock for the 5-day exercise, the tankers flying 30 missions a day. The corresponding bomber exercise was 'Giant Thrust II' held at Andersen AFB, Guam in September of that year during which 14 B-52Ds flew 27 missions a day for 5 days. 'Maple Flag' is a series of exercises in which aircrews from the United States and Canada combine to fly simulated war order missions. SAC B-52s participate in these missions, as they do in Tactical Air Command 'Red Flag' exercises, which are held periodically near Nellis AFB, Nv. 'Busy Brewer' is the name given to the series of exercises which are designed to ensure the B-52's ability to provide a quick and dependable conventional bombing support to NATO theatre

Below: **About to become airborne again on a touch-and-go at Wurtsmith AFB, Mi this B-52G demonstrates a nose down lift-off attitude associated with its end of sortie, light weight.**

Above: **A B-52G of the 2nd Bomb Wing exhibiting the dimensions of the Stratofortress internal weapons bay.**

commanders in Northern Europe. In these exercises, B-52s take off from bases in the north-eastern United States and fly non-stop to Germany and back. Each 18hr flight (supported by air refuelling) includes a simulated bombing run. These exercises are of particular relevance to us here in Europe. Other NATO exercises have included 'Northern Wedding', an exercise over international waters in the North Atlantic in which B-52Gs performed sea reconnaissance/surveillance missions using standard equipment. B-52Ds accomplished two different types of simulated aerial mine laying operations. In 'Autumn Forge', the annual NATO exercise series, SAC aircrews regularly fly high altitude simulated conventional bombing missions over West Germany. 'Giant Voice' is the name given to the annual USAF bombing competition held at Barksdale AFB, La and the B-52s also participate in the equivalent RAF Strike Command competition, for which they deploy to RAF Marham. Other exercises which brought B-52s to England during 1979 were 'Cold Fire',

'Flintlock' and 'Dawn Patrol', while in 1980 there were several detachments from the B-52D Wings visiting UK bases for training in the USAFE area.

Future modifications and the ALCM

Following cancellation of the Rockwell B-1 in 1977, the priority shifted to maximising the B-52's penetration and weapons delivery capability by equipping it with advanced avionics. This work was envisaged in two phases, the second one extending out to 1990. However, following a review of the likely operational life capability of the 20-year old airframes, there is some uncertainty that the full Phase II avionics update will be implemented, an alternative view being that it would be preferable to divert the resultant savings towards a new manned bomber. The more immediate avionics modifications planned for all B-52Gs and Hs are aimed at improving weapons delivery accuracy, further reducing weight through new technology equipment, and substantial reductions in maintenance costs. A total of $323.1 million was requested in the fiscal year 1981 defence budget for B-52 offensive avionics updating, covering 64 aircraft. This included $38.7 million for spares and $45 million for research, development, test and evaluation (RDTE). Flight test of the new avionics was to commence later in 1980, with the first production aircraft planned to be available by September 1981.

The other main B-52 programme imminent is that for modification for the carriage of cruise missiles. All G model aircraft are to be eventually modified to enable them to carry a total of 20 Air Launched

Below: **Dummy Boeing AGM-86B air launched cruise missiles on the starboard wing pylon of a B-52G; the weapons pylons, one either side of the fuselage, will carry six ALCMs each.**
F. B. Mormillo

Cruise Missiles (ALCM), six on each inboard wing pylon and eight on a rotary launcher in the weapons bay. The rotary launcher will also be compatible with the SRAM, and it is envisaged that the ALCM and SRAM will be complementary — both could be carried on some missions.

The ALCM has a turbofan engine and nuclear warhead. It is programmed for precision attack on surface targets, and is extraordinarily accurate. When carried internally in the B-52, the missile's wings and tail will be folded and engine air intake retracted. In November 1977 the Air Force asked Boeing and General Dynamics to build prototype ALCMs, Boeing's design being designated the AGM-86B and General Dynamic's the AGM-109 Tomahawk. After a lengthy review of both weapons, the Air Force selected the Boeing design. In early-April 1980, a $4 billion order was placed with Boeing for the supply of 3,418 of the missiles, to be delivered up to 1989. Accordingly, Boeing will be installing their own brand new missiles in their ageing bombers. It is envisaged that the first ALCM-equipped B-52G unit will become active at Griffiss AFB, NY in December 1982. Initially, the aircraft will be modified for external carriage of ALCMs only, and this first phase should be completed on all B-52Gs by the mid-1980s, with the internal launcher to be installed by the end of the decade. The 1981 budget requests contained $122.4 million for modifications to 40 aircraft for this programme, which included $400,000 for spares and $7 million for RDTE.

It is possible a second generation advanced technology cruise missile will be required in the latter half of the 1980s in view of likely Soviet developments in improving defence capability. In particular, the possibility of a long-range intercepter aircraft which could attack B-52s before they could get into range for launching cruise missiles would dictate a longer-range cruise missile which would enable the bomber to launch the missile outside the operational radius of the Soviet fighter. Another envisaged development centres around Boeing proposals for an improved SRAM, designated SRAM L, which would also incorporate greater range capability over the existing SRAM. It would also have an improved guidance system, and air-to-air capability.

Promising though the ALCM is expected to be, it is seen as being effective against fixed targets only. There will be a continuing need for an effective manned penetration bomber for use against mobile or imprecisely located targets. Initially, the B-52H will soldier on in this role, but there are increasing doubts as to its capabilities in the latter half of the eighties. There must come a time where continued modification of the B-52 will become either impractical or excessively expensive. This has led to

an urgent re-appraisal of the need for a follow-on aircraft, and hopefully it will be a case of third time lucky.

There have been several suggestions as to how best address the problem of the new manned bomber. A modified, stretched, derivative of the F-111/FB-111, termed FB-111B could be available as early as 1986 if an early go-ahead were achieved. This would be a modification of existing FB-111A and F-111D aircraft, and it is a somewhat less ambitious and less expensive programme than the FB-111H proposed some years ago, but is strictly a short term measure. Another possible alternative would be to resurrect the Rockwell B-1 in some form. Although it is accepted that this would be a longer and more expensive programme; it has been estimated that about 100 units could be available by 1987 if a go-ahead was authorised by October 1980. The fourth B-1 is being used in a series of tests to evaluate its survivability in low-level, high speed penetration roles, and includes reprogrammable ECM equipment as well as efforts to generally reduce the radar cross-section. One of the B-1 proposals envisaged a new fixed wing of advanced technology which would give it an unrefuelled range of 8,000 miles at speeds of near Mach 1. Some of the new manned bomber proposals are termed 'Long Range Combat Aircraft'.

The third Rockwell B-1 is to be modified for use in ALCM tests, and the USAF is seeking $30M in 1981 and $51M in 1982 for this programme. This is primarily being seen as an insurance in case the B-52 is not a viable cruise missile carrier; however, the USAF is keeping its options open, and there are also studies to modify B-52Hs as cruise missile carriers in the mid-1980s. This latter requirement could arise in the event of no new manned penetration bomber becoming available.

No matter what way the new manned bomber proposals emerge, it seems almost certain at this stage that there will be B-52s still in the front-line inventory in ten years time. In fact, Boeing has told the USAF that the aircraft is flyable until the year 2000! The aircraft has been one of the most cost-effective weapons systems of all time, and has handsomely outlived all original life projections. Each B-52G averaged about $8 million in cost originally; with successive update and modification programmes, this has now increased several times over, so that each aircraft today represents about $40 million cost. This is a small price to pay for the literally inestimable role the aircraft has played in the maintenance of global peace and the prevention of nuclear conflict. That the aircraft has remained a credible nuclear deterrent over such a long period of time is a tribute both to its original designers and to the ingenuity of US technology in keeping the aircraft viable in a rapidly changing military environment. Much credit is also, of course, due to the personnel in SAC who have maintained the highest levels of proficiency and professionalism consistent with their awesome responsibility.

Current B-52 status

The appendix to this article gives the current disposition of the SAC B-52 fleet. There was a proposal in 1979-80 to close Loring AFB, Me, on cost grounds and distribute the 42nd BW's aircraft to other units, but this decision would appear to have been postponed, if not shelved entirely. In addition to the front-line aircraft, B-52s can still be seen as stored and test aircraft. During a visit to the storage compounds at Davis-Monthan AFB in October 1976, some 150 B-52s were noted, all C, E and F models, and since then the remaining B-52Fs have arrived there, together with such of the D models as did not undergo the Pacer Plank modifications. Interesting aircraft stored at Davis-Monthan are NB-52A 52-0003, which has carried aloft quite a number of experimental craft including the X-15 and the X-24B and M2-F2 lifting bodies (part of the Space Shuttle programme), and 56-0632, an NB-52E, which must rank as the most highly coloured Stratofortress ever. It flew as a Control Configured Vehicle (CCV) with a colour scheme of bright red forward fuselage and tail, engine nacelle trim, wing tanks and fuselage stripe. The CCV embodied Ride Control System which reduced accelerations caused by gust turbulence by up to 30%. Features of the system were horizontal and vertical stabilisers mounted at the front of the B-52. Both these B-52s were parked beside the prototype Boeing 707, and may perhaps be earmarked for preservation?

At least two B-52s have been preserved in museums, both B-52B models; 52-8711 is in the SAC Museum at Offutt AFB, Nb, and 53-0394, named *Lucky Lady 3* is in the USAF Museum at Wright-Patterson AFB, Oh.

Test aircraft still flying include NB-52E 57-0119 with the Air Force Flight Test Center at Edwards AFB, Ca. This is used as a flying engine test bed. Also based at Edwards, at the NASA Dryden Center, is NB-52B NASA 008 (formerly 52-0008). Finally, mention might be made of three B-52Gs noted at Edwards in 1979, 57-6498, 58-0204 and 58-0247, all engaged in the ALCM test programme.

Acknowledgements

Much of the material for this article was gleaned from a visit to the 379th BW at Wurtsmith AFB and from material provided by SAC HQ. We would like to acknowledge the extensive assistance which we received from everyone we met at Wurtsmith.

USAF Strategic Air Command B-52 Units

8th AIR FORCE

19th Air Division

2nd BW	Barksdale AFB, La.	62nd BS	B-52G
		596nd BS	B-52G
7th BW	Carswell AFB, Tx	9th BS	B-52D
		20th BS	B-52D

40th Air Division

379th BW	Wurtsmith AFB, Mi	524th BS	B-52G
410th BW	K. I. Sawyer AFB, Mi	644th BS	B-52H

42nd Air Division

19th BW	Robins AFB, Ga	28th BS	B-52G
68th BW	Seymour-Johnson AFB, NC	51st BS	
			B-52G
97th BW	Blytheville AFB, Ar	340th BS	B-52G

45th Air Division

42nd BW	Loring AFB, Me	69 BS	B-52G
416th BW	Griffiss AFB, NY	668th BS	B-52G

15th AIR FORCE

4th Air Division

28th BW	Ellsworth AFB, SD	37th BS	B-52H
		77th BS	B-52H

12th Air Division

22nd BW	March AFB, Ca	2nd BS	B-52D
96th BW	Dyess AFB, Tx	337th BS	B-52D

14th Air Division

93rd BW	Castle AFB, Ca*	328th BS	B-52G/H
320th BW	Mather AFB, Ca	441st BS	B-52G

47th Air Division

92nd BW	Fairchild AFB, Wa	325th BS	B-52G

57th Air Division

5th BW	Minot AFB, ND	23rd BS	B-52H
319th BW	Grand Forks AFB, ND	46th BS	B-52H

OVERSEAS UNIT

3rd Air Division

43rd SW	Andersen AFB, Guam	60th BS	B-52D

*Also at Castle is the 4017th Combat Crew Training Squadron which gives instruction to all B-52G/H crews

Right: **At sortie's end a B-52G lands under a late-afternoon sky, in this instance at RAF Marham during the Strike Command Bombing and Navigation Competition.**

Above: **A classic view of a B-52D showing the camouflage pattern on the aircraft's upper surfaces.** *Boeing*